i

Cracking Pluto

Spiritual astrology
Volume II

astrology and reincarnation

by Sebastian van Wingerden

Lillalith publications

Cracking Pluto

Spiritual astrology
Volume II

by S.C.W. van Wingerden

ISBN 9789080715592
first edition May 2017

cover: S.C.W. van Wingerden
© S.C.W. van Wingerden

Lillalith publications

www.lillalith.com

CONTENT

Forword 1

Planet Pluto 4

Cracking Pluto 8

Pluto in the first house 21

Pluto in the second house 33

Pluto in the third house 46

Pluto in the fourth house 57

Pluto in the fifth house 67

Pluto in the sixth house 78

Pluto in the seventh house 89

Pluto in the eighth house 100

Pluto in the ninth house 111

Pluto in the tenth house 123

Pluto in the eleventh house 133

Pluto in the twelfth house 144

Foreword

Pluto is a controversial Planet. Not long ago the NASA declared Pluto as a non-planet causing confusion about its mere existence. That is typical Pluto: it hits you in your sheer existence. No nonsense: Pluto is a celestial body and belongs to astrology.

Pluto was discovered in 1930 and is not yet really understood. For more than twenty years in my profession as an astrologer I have studied the effects of Pluto on people's life. By listening well to the responses and life stories of my clients the picture became clear. That's what I love about being an astrologer. All those amazing life stories. Since my way of reading is spiritual dealing with the evolution of the soul, Pluto always was highlighted in my readings building up a tremendous amount of data about this planet. I started to give reincarnation sessions in 1998 and the Plutonic themes of past life experiences of each individual were unfolded for me. What a miracle. It is really true.

In 1993 I was introduced to the spiritual astrology of Carteret. It deals with the reason why we are born and how to get enlightened. Pluto plays a crucial role in it. Cracking Pluto is an important turning point. It caught my heart and I stuck to it. In 2008 I published a book about this way of reading 'The northern Moon node the message from beyond', ISBN 978-90-807155-85. However Pluto is not exclusively part of the system of Carteret. Pluto is universal. As a celestial body Pluto has an astral influence on earth no matter your astrology approach. Pluto is Pluto.

You have got malefics and benefics. Malefics are the hard planets and the benefics are the mellow planets of love and joy. Mars and Saturn are notorious malefics. Pluto can be added in this group. Once you know the traps of Pluto you don't get trapped by it anymore. That is what you gain. When I explain all the dirty tricks and manipulations of Pluto don't call me an advertiser of evil but turn it to your advantage. Don't get mad at me when you read something about yourself that you don't want to know. Don't kill the messenger. Throwing the book against the wall anger won't help. Knowing yourself is not always easy.

Especially when you are between the ages of thirty and forty years old this book can be useful to pull you through the Pluto crisis. Always, at any age, it is helpful to understand someone else's Pluto problem.

From the author, Sebastian van Wingerden.

Planet Pluto

Pluto is not a planet. Pluto is a celestial body. Pluto is part of the Kuiper belt. Behind the gas planets (Jupiter to Neptune) there is a belt made of billions of small material objects, called the Kuiper belt. Those objects are balls of dust and ice. Astronomers call them dirty snowballs. Pluto is one of them.

Pluto is one of those dirty snowballs and a very special one too.

1) He is the biggest of all until now and the closest to the sun.

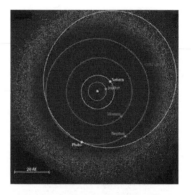

2) Pluto's orbit is out of line with the ecliptic. They meet at an angle of about 15 degrees.

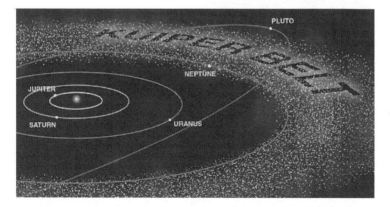

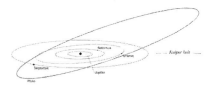

3) On top of that Pluto is orbiting the sun in a grand ellipse. Most distant, at its aphelion, he is twice as far from the sun as he is when he is closest to the sun, at his perihelion, just as close as Neptune is.

This all is very peculiar and one might wonder whether Pluto collided in the past with another dirty snowball and got knocked out of orbit. This is the main theory of Pluto's history. Colliding objects are a common thing in the solar system and in the Kuiper belt too. Collided objects from the Kuiper belt are called comets. They fall out of the Kuyper belt into an orbit meeting the Sun, losing some of their mass by each turn around. In the end they vanish. The most famous is comet Halley. Pluto however is not a comet. He survived the collision. He did not fall into the Sun. He only got into a very eccentric orbit. The fact Pluto survived its collision is very symbolic for the nature of Pluto's influence. It explains its fighting nature.

Pluto is very small, a bit smaller than the earth. Pluto has a huge satellite, Charon, being much more larger than the earthly moon. Pluto might be considered a double planet. Charon is known in Roman mythology as being the boatman carrying you over the river Styx to the aftermath (heaven or hell) after your death. How appropriate. It was not the astrologers who gave Pluto and Charon its name. This all explains the dualistic, paradoxical and extreme features of Pluto.

5

Pluto and Charon by Hubble

Pluto's eccentric orbit around the Sun means its pace in the Zodiac changes over time. When he is close to the Sun he goes fast and when he is far away he goes slow. In Scorpio (at its perihelion) Pluto goes three degrees per year and in Taurus (at its aphelion) only one.

This means the moment transit Pluto squares natal Pluto differs a lot depending on when you are born. When you are born in the 1960's or 70's you get this square when you are 36 years old and when you are born around 2070 the square occurs in your 89th year.

Birth year 1-1-....	Transit Pluto square natal Pluto	
1920	(1974)	54th year
1930	(1979)	49th
1940	(1984)	44th
1950	(1990)	40th
1960	(1996)	36th
1970	(2006)	36th
1980	(2019)	39th
1990	(2033)	43rd
2000	(2051)	51st
2010	(2069)	59th
2020	(2088)	68th

2030	(2105)	75th
2040	(2121)	81st
2050	(2137)	87th
2060	(2148)	88th
2070	(2159)	89th
2080	(2169)	89th
2090	(2178)	88th
2100	(2186)	86th
2110	(2192)	82nd

This would mean a native born in 2110 will crack Pluto during his 82th year. That seems to me a bit late even if the average life expectancy would be 120 or 130 years in those times. How natives with Pluto in Taurus will crack Pluto is a mystery. The theory is they crack Pluto during its half square. Also some main transits could trigger the trick.

Cracking Pluto

Pluto represents the underworld. Nobody knows what is hidden under the ground. What you don't know is queer. Suppose the underworld collapses. You slide away with it down under the ground. That is not what you want and you do everything you can to prevent such a calamity. That's the Plutonic energy. Pluto is about power. Who gets who down. Pluto is about extremes. Driven by fear or ambition you fall into extremes. Either you go for it with all your might or you hold in. There is no middle way. Whereas Saturn can be considered as a break and Mars as a brake pedal Pluto is both. Hitting the gas and pulling the breaks at the same time causing a cramp in your body.

In your lifespan Plutonic problems are growing and growing. They reach their maximum when transit Pluto makes its square with your natal Pluto. It starts three years before when transit Pluto enters its eighth degree orb with natal Pluto. Most people crack their Plutonic fears between the age of 33 and 40. The constraint will be transformed into pure positive energy. Some people crack Pluto later and a lot of people never manage to crack him. Cracking Pluto is a continuous thing. You have got to stay alert with Pluto. Unceasingly you are challenged to do it right each time in a higher degree.

Pluto as an astral influence is pure existential survival energy. Plutonic energies are sheer power, a giant force deep within you. Pluto is both an inner drive and a huge paralyzing fear to do so. Pluto is a potential atom bomb inside yourself. Pluto is a wormhole you get sucked into. Unconsciously you are afraid this atom bomb will go off in an uncontrolled way. So you suppress this power and you try to control it. Nobody notices your anger or fear because you hide it. This control is the agony of Pluto. The split is: the more you try to control it, the higher the chance the calamity will happen. Pluto is a notorious sick maker, a deadly one. Its energies are felt very physically. It works out as a physical cramp. Cracking Pluto is like cracking a nut, your own nut, your own suit of armor.

Basically Pluto is a power 'too big to handle', especially in the first forty years of your life. It becomes a shield of self-protection. Breaking down this shield is cracking Pluto. When you crack Pluto its energy becomes manageable. Basic rule: *stay calm under any circumstances*. The point is: how to stay relaxed without downers. Basically any Pluto problem is an emotional problem. Scorpio is a water sign. After cracking Pluto you are able to stay calm and show a proper sense of perspective. The only way to learn how to stay calm and do the right thing is in the heat of the moment.

Pluto is an irrational fear creeping into you when you suspect something very important is going to go incredibly wrong. You smell problems and you want to prevent it. A tension is building up constraining your demeanor. Hellish fantasies about worst case scenarios are troubling your mind. In such a state you actually don't know anymore what you are doing. Something is taking over your common sense, your presence of mind. Pluto is a funnel of restricted awareness. Pluto is a kind of paranoia, a breathtaking whirlpool taking away your self-control. You are afraid 'the whole world will turn against you and you surely will be finished off'. The features are: cold sweat, shivering, panicking, yelling, outbursts of anger and violence,

9

stomach cramps, spasms, nail biting, nervous breakdowns, bowing and apologizing, feeling paralyzed and more of those things. Or you may fall ill. An incurable disease no doctor understands strikes you and that becomes your Plutonic survival battle.

Plutonic forces are too big to handle. As a consequence you either overreact like a great dictator or you do nothing like a lame duck. If the fear is greater you control yourself and you hold in. If the power is greater you overreact. The real control is gone and the conditions are created for the calamity to happen. The calamity you fear so much happens like a self-fulfilling prophecy. That is a pattern. Each time it goes that way.

Pluto is authority thinking. Authority thinking is based on fear of sabotage and punishment. As a double planet Pluto represents the authority both inside and outside. The outside authority is the public opinion, God, the legislation, your parents, the doctor, a high official and anyone you consider as an authority. Who is the boss? The inside authority is yourself, your own set of standards. Pluto is the split between the two. Pluto's drive is to fulfill a cosmic ideal image. An imaginary authority inside you is demanding so. 'This is how it ought to be'. To you it is a self-evident truth. You get upset when you see it is not shared and a distress sets in. All trust fades away. The fear sets in and you are sucked into a funnel. Either you stand up and revolt or you hold in with a grudge: It's not fair....... but never ever fight the authorities because you'll be hanged.

There is no way to understand Pluto rationally. There is no logic in Pluto. Pluto as the ruler of a water sign is based on emotions. If you try to explain your Plutonic drives and fears in a logical way you get stuck. With a triumphal smile your conversation partner will point out to you that you are a rambler. Pluto is an irrational fear. You are shocked by an event an outsider wouldn't be bothered by. Why is it worrying you so much? Why do you get in such distress? Why does it touch you so deeply? It is not to be explained rationally. It is not really possible to name it. It is inexplicable. That is why talking doesn't help. Discussions only stiffen up the differences. On the other hand if you try to correct someone's Pluto behavior you'll bounce your head into a wall. You won't get through. Beware to give lectures about Pluto. Suddenly someone stands up red hot, yelling, cursing and opposing. I have heard: "What you say is not true. I have Pluto in the fifth house and I don't have any problem with children. I have had three abortions and I don't care at all." That's Pluto.

The only way to understand Pluto is by past lives. In one or more past lives a calamity occurred around the themes of the house of Pluto's position. When this theme is triggered an enormous drive and fear pops up not to get in the same situation again or to do it better this time. Mostly those calamities had to do with murder, war, torture, prisons, treachery, cruel despotism, unfair punishment, long lasting situations of isolation and total unhappiness without hope and so on. Sometimes there is regret about having done something wrong. In this life you don't want to make the same mistake again.

Pluto is an invisible force pushing you into awkward situations you remember from past lives. With Pluto you create your own hell. Pluto is a devil. It takes a devil to beat the devil. Once you have defeated the devil (on his own terms) you come into your power. Now that you know how to handle the ways of evil you have cracked Pluto and you will be transformed into an angel. But the devil never gives up. So you have to defeat him again and again. You have to crack Pluto again and again. Once you fall asleep he has got you. Is this a tunnel vision or is it real?

Your Plutonic fears create the circumstances for a calamity like a self-fulfilling prophecy. The calamity repeats itself unless you change your attitude. When you are afraid of a dog the dog will smell it. He will approach exactly you and not someone else. He comes up close to you growling and showing his sharp teeth. Standing there you shiver imaging how he will bite you and rip you into parts. After all he did not do it. He was playing around with your fears. But if you get down to it, it was you who got so extremely afraid. Why? You can't explain. It is the Plutonic heritage from past lives. Life is not meant to have those fears. Pluto's intention is to overcome it, to break out of this pattern. You can compare it with a car accident. After the crash you are afraid to drive a car again. The only way to get rid of those fears is to get back behind the steering wheel. It seems a cruel pattern of the cosmos to send you back into your fears but it is not.

The great Plutonic split is: *you have to do exactly what you are so afraid of and you are freed.* Plutonic fears are deep inside your soul. It is in yourself. You cannot blame someone else for it. You are born with those fears. As long as you blame the outer world for your Plutonic problems the battle once begun continues. The moment you crack Pluto is the moment you can see for yourself how you overreact. At the end of the tunnel is the light. Calmness sets in and you let go or you do with the same serenity exactly what you have got to do. Caress that dog!

When you overcome your Plutonic fears your soul makes a quantum leap in strength and wisdom. Cracking Pluto is the karmic transformation of the soul. It cleans out a sickness in your soul, the memories of cruelties in past lives. It means the end of all wars and a start up to paradise. It is a heavy process because it goes much further than a superficial change of behavior or viewpoints. It is not a fancy new style you adopt to be more popular or more successful. It is a return to your source. Some kind of disease inside your soul dies out. The fear and anger is transformed into self-assurance, peace of mind and wisdom. A lot of positive energy will be freed.

In childhood the Plutonic energies, fears and drives, come out freely and unrestrained, unconscious, pure and without a plan. But the Plutonic energies are fierce. First the parents and later school will put a check on it. Power collisions and misunderstandings will take place. The fierceness is in the child. The child loses the confrontation and becomes afraid and frustrated. The power becomes a fear. The process of suppressing the Plutonic energies sets in. The child swallows his discontent. He starts holding in his energies. He does not show them anymore. The fear for troubles prevails.

No matter how you hide it for a lot of people your fears are obvious. When you are funneled in it is easy to manipulate you because you can't come to the point. They find tricks to abuse your fears. Those people will find you like the dog mentioned above. They fuck you up and you bite. You make a mistake, lose the discussion and they tell you how to behave and what to do. Your Plutonic energies are canned into compulsory behavior. A tension of discontent sets in, builds up, becomes bigger and bigger until transit Pluto squares your natal Pluto. Then the balloon explodes. The atom bomb goes off. You cannot hold in anymore and you just let go. Eventually Pluto is a force not to be stopped by nothing and nobody. The dikes break through and you lose all control over your life. In this period you actually think you die. You have got to give up a lot of things, big things: your family, your job, your wife and above all your security, your basis. All the things which used to be so important for you. Sometimes you fall ill and you find yourself defenseless. Misfortunes never come singly. It does not rain. It pours. You go through your basic existential fears and you crack Pluto. A new reality is created. The sun will shine again twice its size.

Roughly there are two ways Pluto might manifest itself. Or the drive is bigger than the fear and you rush into problems again and again. Or the opposite happens and you don't dare to say or do anything. You run away from it or you act like an obedient slave.
Cracking Pluto also roughly manifests itself in two ways. Either you crack Pluto yourself and you finally go where you always ran away from. Or you are forced by the circumstances and overpowered by the situation.

If the drive is bigger than the fear you try to control the situation. You make sure you don't make mistakes and you get what you are aiming for. Not getting it is a calamity with hate, despair or terrible self-blame as a result. Again and again you rush into a stressful situation with a tremendous amount of energy. You can achieve astonishing results with those fighting energies. You can get mighty rich and of high position. The older you get, the more you grow in your power. Everybody looks up to you. But success based on Plutonic energies won't last. Eventually you get exhausted or you will find a final adversary to tackle you. You win, you win and you win until you find your Waterloo during cracking Pluto. Eventually your domination will not be tolerated and you collapse. You meet someone who rips apart all your manipulation tactics and the calamity happens. You are dethroned. Someone else has taken over the situation and it is over. You have got no support. You get fired, your spouse walks away, your business partner disappears with the money or other terrible things like that. It happens and you have to take the consequences. You think: 'This is the end. I am finished off. Nothing I can do anymore.' But despite all the next day you wake up again and you have to go on through. You fall into a crisis causing a deep change in yourself. You rearrange your life. You realise how it happened, you accept it and you crack Pluto a lot wiser than before. It will not happen to you next time. You can also keep on grouching but that is not cracking Pluto.

Even if you win your Waterloo you eventually get confronted with the same question. Why are you so tense? What are you constantly controlling and manipulating for? Does this make you happy? Eventually not. You get tired. You decide to crack Pluto yourself and quit yourself creating a new future. You don't want to prove yourself anymore. You have already proven yourself. You are already high and dry. You don't need it anymore. A psychological crisis sets in and you crack Pluto yourself. Some hang-ups transform and you return to a more human and soft approach. Back to normal.

If the fear is bigger than the drive, you hold in with Pluto and you don't dare to stand for yourself. You are not free. You live how you are told to and you don't follow your will. You constantly get overruled and you wind up in a situation you do not want. You try to do your best but you don't get the recognition. You might be married with somebody you do not like anymore but a divorce is out of the question. Your work is not satisfying and you don't do anything. Somehow you get stuck because of your blockades. Your life becomes dull. You become a nobody. You long for a change but don't know how. You are upset and hold in bursting with emotion. During cracking Pluto you get on your plate what you always wanted to avoid. Walking away and holding in is not an option anymore. For years you were afraid your wife would leave you and then she does. Or with your work: finally you are fired. This way you are forced by the situation to go through your Pluto fears. And that is only good.

The other way of cracking Pluto is you make the changes yourself. The discontent grows and grows until the bomb goes off. You simply can't go anymore and you crack Pluto yourself. You change your attitude and you learn to say no. Or you finally go for the job or the woman you longed for. Finally you dare to do it. This means you have to give up a lot of things.

Cracking Pluto almost always comes at the most inconvenient moment. That hits the hardest. You already thought you were drowning by all your problems and then suddenly, BANG, you get the final shot. 'You picked the right time to leave me Joanne ....' You never thought she'd do that. Your last security leaves you. There is no plan for cracking Pluto. It happens to you. You have to crack Pluto in your daily life. Cracking Pluto is done in the moment itself. The cosmos decides for you when to crack Pluto. It is not up to you to choose the moment of cracking Pluto.

Cracking Pluto is hard, especially in the beginning. It is like dying. But in the end you are liberated from the yoke or dependence on Joanne. Of course it will last some years until your life is rearranged but the beginning is made. Later you meet more Joanne types, for karmic reasons, but now after having cracked Pluto for the first time, you know how to handle them. Cracking Pluto is a continuous process. The first time is the hardest. After the first time your Plutonic fears will be triggered again and again but now you can recognise it.

Cracking Pluto yourself means you have to say yes to new opportunities. For example: you have always been an obedient clerk and you are offered a promotion with a lot of responsibility. You always avoided any responsibility and the cold sweat breaks out by the mere thought on it. Still you have to say 'yes'. Or you are in the forties living alone for years and you fall in love again. No matter how queer you have to go for it. You have to show. Suddenly you get what you always missed and you again run away from it? It is like dying. But you have to follow your will, your own authority. Saying 'no' means your spirituality will die. If you dare to do it you will find out to your surprise how easy it was. Just show up. The only question remains: 'Why didn't I do it before? What was holding me back?'

Cracking Pluto is like dying. Dying is to release and let go. Let go of all your resistance to the cosmic will. Let go of all your fake certainties you are clinging to. Just give it up and it is the end of all your problems. Mostly cracking Pluto comes in the form of some kind of calamity waking you up. During this calamity you have the feeling that you die. You might get sick literally. The square of transiting Pluto and natal Pluto is overwhelming. The split is: Coping with the things you fear the most means you have got to do the things you fear the most. When you survive it, and you will, you are released from your irrational fears. While you are in your twenties you simply lack the power or experience.

The only way of cracking Pluto is to make a firm decision: the next time I will rise up and follow my heart. Or: I won't work for Maggie's farm no more. And you stick to it. Some talking with an advisor or doing some healing sessions will help. Eventually you have to do it yourself. You jump and you do exactly what you have always been afraid of. During cracking Pluto you will find out that all your fears were fully unjustified and the door for real happiness is opened. Finally you are freed. Eventually you and your Pluto are your own authority and nobody rules over you. Cracking Pluto starts with a firm decision and you hold yourself on that decision. A tremendous amount of energy is freed to do things you never thought you were able to.

Cracking Pluto is choosing for a new situation. However the moment you quit and leave the old situation there is no new reality yet. The old concept is dead but there is no new one yet or only an experimental one. That is the problem. There is no certainty to hold onto yet. That is the fear. It is like jumping into the black hole of the unknown. It is like throwing away all your safety belts without having new ones. Your ego wants safety and certainty.

You always have the freedom to refuse to crack Pluto. You don't have to. "What," you might reason, "I don't want to die, I am not crazy. I am not throwing my securities away." However if you don't you will die regardless. You will die a spiritual death. If you don't die before you die, you rot away. Cracking Pluto is to rejuvenate yourself. If you don't you will be cramping up more and more. You'll become an old nagging fox. You get sour and discontent in perpetual strife. Or your life gets dull reducing you to a plant. You can get a mysterious sickness although you think you have got it all made. Pluto is a notorious sick maker. All the suppressed energies get in a knot and reveal themselves as a sickness, a serious sickness, almost incurable like Cancer and so on. Somewhere in the body those energies cling together and you get sick. The list of Ebertine is a useful tool to find out whether your disease is Plutonic or not. When you crack Pluto your disease will be cured. At least the psychological cause of the disease will be cured. I hope you don't mind me preaching hell and doom when you don't crack Pluto. But it is never too late to crack Pluto. The door to crack Pluto is always open no matter how long you wait.

When you crack Pluto for the first time you solve karma from past lives that blocked you in your personal growth. The road is opened to future expansions. In the beginning it is very insecure but as the times go by your situation will improve, expand and stabilize. It still will last some years to get rooted in the new reality. It still lasts a while until all old fears are fully washed away. In return you get a higher knowledge. You gain cosmic insight and a deep trust in yourself. After the big bang of cracking Pluto you made a grand swap, a quantum leap, in your consciousness. Finally you are a real grown-up. You will experience a relaxation in your body and in your aura giving free way to a warm and understanding approach. You soften up. That is not weakness. On the contrary, it is power and compassion. Power combined with a higher mind. When you give this power a free ride you gain appreciation. You are simply a much nicer person. You are much more happy and people feel it. In return you get what you want, although it still takes some years to pick the fruits and to count the results.

After cracking Pluto you will win all your Plutonic confrontations. You are able to stay calm under any circumstances and handle the situation nicely no matter what. Your power is changed into cosmic power of wisdom. It gives you the horn of plenty, the cornucopia. Everything you touch will be changed into gold. All the astral qualities from Neptune to the Moon will join the Pluto transformation and will radiate in a positive way. Beware to stay alert. Stay in tune with the cosmos. Pluto has to be cracked continuously. You will continually meet situations on your path checking out your cosmic power. The moment you forget and fall asleep you get in the tunnel-funnel again. The moment the worries of your ego take over again, you fall. The last time to crack Pluto is at your physical death. Let's hope that will be the easiest.

Some people get a try out of their cracking Pluto when transit Pluto makes a half square with their natal Pluto. Then they get a taste of what their cracking of Pluto will be about on a larger scale and which part of the horn of plenty will be their part.

Pluto in the signs is not an individual quality. It is a generation sign. Pluto in the signs is used for mundane astrology.

Pluto in the first house

With Pluto in the first house your Plutonic drives and fears are purely existential. It is all about basic instincts. You have a strong sense of independence. There is a general existential fear to go under. Somehow, under your skin, you feel you have no right to live. There are hidden enemies everywhere. Pluto in the first house feels like a sudden attack is hanging in the air forcing you to fight for your life. There are potential murderers around every corner. You have got a strong survival instinct. To be or not to be. You feel unprotected. You stand alone. You are all alone in a dangerous and hostile world without support. Among those fears you are very courageous. When you set yourself a goal, you accomplish it. If not you fear the death penalty. So you make sure you don't lose.

A lot of natives with Pluto in the first house have a big mouth. If the drive is bigger you intimidate and bluff to eliminate any opposition in advance. You imagine the worst case scenario and you set out to beat it off. When someone points out to you that you are mistaken, you think it's the end of the world and you go for your defence. The best defence is an attack.

On the other hand you've got the silent types. Out of fear you act like a nondescript person making sure to pass all the tests and to get your career. You retreat and prepare yourself before you go. That's the best guarantee not to lose.

Natives with Pluto in the first house are bad losers. Criticism is a declaration of war. So they make sure to do everything right. They seem to have a great personality but in reality they need a lot of support. When you get to know them better they are like putty in your hands as long as you give them the confirmation they need. Physically they are very uptight as if they've got the finger on the trigger. Pluto works out physically and with Pluto in the first house this is squared. The Plutonic stress on basic instincts also stretches out onto the sexual plane. You don't take 'no' for an answer and you keep on pushing until you've got her. A rejection is considered a calamity. The silent types might be afraid of the other sex and don't even dare to approach the opposite sex for the same fear of rejection.

The irrational and inexplicable existential fears of Pluto in the first house stem from one or more past lives. You died in a fierce fight. You were killed in an unequal fight. The Bhagavad Gītā describes a situation where war is inevitable. The enemy persists in its intention to destroy you. The only thing left is to prepare yourself and defend yourself as well as possible whether you want it or not. You don't let them slaughter you off just like that. But you did not stand a chance and you were slaughtered off. Or you had a past life of being overpowered by the mafia or by a group of villagers. Or you were a simple farmer and one day a bunch of knights came along telling you that you were not supposed to live there setting all the houses in the community on fire. Desperately you fought against all odds for your house, wife and child but you were brutally kicked and stabbed to death. The split is: you were not afraid during the fight. In the fight itself you fought blindly giving yourselves totally. The fear came after the fight when you realised what had happened. Another issue is: it was not unexpected. For years the threat and intimidation was going on and then suddenly it happened. You weren't always the loser. I remember a man with Pluto in the first house who was a leader of a mighty Arabian tribe. His allies found out he was in love with a woman from another tribe. Her father rejected this marriage. For reasons of pride he had to declare war otherwise he would lose respect. He won all his battles but not that woman. She was tortured for the misfortune she brought over her tribe, which was actually her father's doing. Women with Pluto in the first house might remember lives in wartime caring for the wounded and eventually being bombed out themselves. Being born with Pluto in the first house means past life memories of a merciless war. The conclusion is: living on earth is eternal war. They hate it but … you can't get around it. That's the split. Eventually after cracking Pluto you realize it is not the case.

Young children with Pluto in the first house are often very independent. They like to go their own way. They want to go out and discover. They are very direct. If parents put a check on their impulses a Pluto in the first house child will react hot tempered to defend his freedom and territory. And they will get their payback. They do all kinds of things they are much too small for not yet knowing what dangers are lurking out there. So continuously on all kind of initiatives they are put under control. They are pushed out of their own willpower. This triggers their Plutonic drive, their basic instinct to fight for their territory. The clashes continue and eventually the child surrenders. The child begins to repress its own impulses. 'Will I do it or not', becomes the question and initially he freezes. A tension is built up in the body on these moments of hesitation. They have a lot of physical energy. Holding back they suppress this energy and eventually their body becomes a hard tense rock.

When Pluto in the first house children do something wrong it is very difficult to point out to them that they are mistaken. They will react emotionally. They will get red hot, start to yell and throw things at your head. They throw a major tantrum and don't stop screaming. They throw themselves on the ground as if they were murdered as a past life memory. They go completely berserk. At that moment they experience some kind of death penalty. They think this is it, now my life is over. Finished. If you respond as a loving parent and ask: "Why do you get so upset? I don't mind you making a mistake. I love you anyway," they won't hear it in that moment. Later they cannot explain why they lost control, not even when they have calmed down. If you see a Pluto in first house child floundering and doing stupid things you don't say: "No, you stupid kid, you are totally wrong!", because your child will overreact. You should handle them with silk gloves. Later on, after the event, you might show and teach them how to do it properly. The danger is when the parent gets sucked into the Plutonic energies of the child and loses his or her patience. When you as a parent get angry, start yelling back and show your child the hard way, the fear and inner protest will only escalate. Especially when in the turmoil of the moment, the child gets beaten and is punished hard.

Natives with Pluto in the first house feel like they are under attack by the slightest disapproval. They need a lot of confirmation. Basically they want to be the best. Every confrontation is a matter of life and death. Often they are fanatic and excellent sportsmen. They always want to win. Sport is a good way for them to release their fighting energies. On the other hand there is a big problem: they are bad losers. Nobody likes that. If they lose they expect the electric chair. But that is the learning process: 'Although you are not the best, you still are still pretty good'. I remember a four year old boy with Pluto in the first who was good at playing chess. He loved it but when he was losing a game he threw the chessboard through the room and the whole family was joking about how he was such a bad loser. Half a year later I met him again and asked him he had learned to be a good loser. After a deep thought he admitted, he still was not able to lose. They are able to accomplish a lot of things but losing, no. Give them the credits and they are like putty in your hands.

The split of Pluto in the first house is that you have a drive to be independent and at the same time you need confirmation. You behave like you don't need anyone but at the same time you need a lot of approval and admiration, especially from your partner. They need at least one person to be number one for. They need to have respect and admiration. Nobody knows this because it is well hidden. It is unconscious. But natives with Pluto in the first house feel it every day. They make sure that these insecurities remain unseen. Don't you think they are weak. Criticism is met fiercely. You're either on my team or out. If you are not with me you are against me. You want to be patted on your back for your abilities. You've got the silent types, they are smarter, but generally this admiration is won by showing off behaviour, intimidation and bragging. All to get allies. Some men play the macho game to the maximum. One insult and you suffer a terrible revenge. Some have a bad reputation. They are afraid of you. Don't mess around with that man. Don't start an argument with that guy, he won't give in.

But don't get intimidated by natives with Pluto in the first house. They create a fake image of greatness. The silent types get their admiration by an impressive list of results.

That's not fake. They don't need to yell. They are too intelligent for that. Still they make sure they are untouchable. Remember: If this guy is on your side you have got a strong ally. For the mutual support.

Some natives with Pluto in the first house suffer phobias. Fears of mice, of the police, of the mafia, of men in general and many more, travelling incognito in blinded cars as a defence against any possible assault. Once I did a hypnosis session with a woman tracing back her mysterious fears about power and sexuality. When she was young she had a panic attack when she heard footsteps at the entrance of her flat. As usual I began the session with a relaxation exercise and I asked her to face her fears. She had no troubles relaxing and said: "Me, afraid? I am not afraid of anybody or anything. I can handle everything!" I focussed her on the footsteps and, yes, there she was in a past life. She heard the footsteps. The door was opened and they took her up and brought her to a madhouse where she was locked up in an empty room. Naked and forgotten she died of starvation. That was her specific past life memory of how she was not allowed to be.

With Pluto in the first house you often have a problem with one or more colleagues. One clash and the paranoia pops up. No matter how hard you try to hide you feel threatened, in the long run it will become obvious. Although you try to keep cool and you hold in your fears as much as possible, one menacing gesture, an angry sigh or a look of reproach easily escapes. Even if you behave in a correct way you feel the tension under your skin. It will be noticed.
Pluto in the first house means you need a lot of independence in your job. You should have your own company

to be your own boss and be free in your decisions. If you have a supervisor or boss, you need a lot of freedom. Tell a native with Pluto in the first house, "get it done no matter how", and they'll do it. With their fighting spirit they are very able to reach the top. Once they set themselves a goal they won't give up. They give themselves totally. They are come back kids. Everybody thinks: "Wow, what a guy. See how dedicated and committed he is." But it is pure self-image. It's a blown up ego. Cracking Pluto they either collapse, find their final adversary or simply do not want to be a leader anymore. All those harsh confrontations, all those tensions, all those pitfalls .....

With Pluto in the first house you suffer your biggest fears in a relationship. You look for a partner who is totally and unconditionally yours. Without a partner you are nothing. When your partner doesn't support you anymore you are lost. With your partner you meet your real self. So for your partner you do make concessions. You cannot hide your basic fears from your partner. You are like putty in the hands of your spouse no matter how strong and independent you come across as. You need a partner for the confirmation to be. Even worse, some natives with Pluto in the first house are very submissive in a relationship. The existential fears are overwhelming and you reduce yourself to nothing in order to get support. Nobody knows it. In public you keep up appearances. They are totally dependent, first at their parent's home and later in their marriage. The crisis comes when the partner dies or runs away. In rare cases natives with Pluto in the first house stay single. Nineteen nine percent live together. All on your own you don't feel safe. So you make sure you get a partner to support you. If the relationship ends you immediately start another one because you cannot do without. Some natives with Pluto in the first house go for a partner weaker than themselves. A wife who looks up to him. A husband who eats out of your hand. If not, you will push on until he will. Eventually this won't last. It is an unequal relationship. By the time of cracking Pluto you find out your spouse is of no support, a millstone around your neck, not able to keep up with you and jealous too.

Natives with Pluto in the first house have a strong sexual drive. This is another reason to need a relationship. The physical tensions have to be released with sex. You simply have got to have sex. One might think: 'Great, that is exactly the lover I am dreaming of'. But when you have had enough sex and want to stop it might get to be a problem. It is taken as a personal insult and a total rejection. That might become a problem: all those struggles in bed. I remember a woman having a consultation about her husband with Pluto in the first house. He was not just a somebody, he was a psychology teacher at a state university and very well mannered. At night in bed however, he turned into a sex maniac. During the intercourse he lost all contact doing his thing. He was taking out his physical tensions on her like a robot. She felt like she was being raped. She tried to discuss his behaviour over and over again but in vain. Either he denied it or he promised to change. But he did not change. What could she do? Also women can be that demanding. Without sex you are not a man neither woman. That's the tension.

People with Pluto in the first house keep on pushing until they have got the partner they want. When you fall in love with somebody with Pluto in the first house you initially think: 'Gee, what a stud, is there anything he can't do?' But later on you find out the opposite is true. He or she totally needs your approval. He is claiming your love. You are expected to give him your full support in everything he does. What a bummer. Especially when you originally thought: 'Wow, that man will be my safe haven for the rest of my life'. But without your support and dedication he does not make it. He completely depends on you. He can't even bake his own eggs. It takes years to find out.

When transit Pluto squares your natal Pluto all your tensions and fears will come to a climax. Transiting Pluto is passing the fourth house, so the transformation is felt in your family life. The time has come for total independence. You handle your things your way and your spouse hers. For the better. If it goes well your spouse will be freed in supporting you all the time being your second mate. The relationship will improve. But often one of the two doesn't understand the signals on the wall. Finally your spouse does not accept your claiming behaviour anymore. She says: "I won't do your dirty laundry anymore. I am not your secretary. I am going to do my own things. Help yourself!" She had told you a hundred times before and now the divorce is a fact. She leaves you after all those years. You are kicked out. Or he says: "I have been supporting you all my life and you keep on asking for more? Enough is enough." Throughout the years he realized the relationship has changed into a mutual nagging instead of a mutual support.

Cracking Pluto in the first house is all about divorce. If you choose yourself for divorce you crack Pluto yourself. For years already your spouse stopped confirming you. After all those years you found out there is nothing your spouse can add to you. After thousands of fights and nervous breakdowns (giving in again) you realise you are better off without. And then you jump. It's your decision to get a divorce. A peculiar story is a man with Pluto in the first house who came to me because of his belly aches after he ended his relationship. The man had three master degrees and a magnificent job as a top lawyer. His partner was 13 years younger with no education and from another country. She was very jealous, always suspecting him of cheating on her. After 8 years he realized the basis of his love was to help her out as he always helped everybody out. And who was helping him? Nobody. Only problems. He sent her away and since then he got those mysterious belly aches. He felt like a living death. He was the former Arabian chief mentioned earlier and she was the woman of that other tribe. This knowledge helped him understand why he had to go through this relationship: The relationship had no meaning anymore. The only way to end his longing in vain and his guild feelings is to have this experience.

When divorce sets in it feels like dying. Now you are on your own. You have to bake your own eggs. You might get mysteriously sick and no doctor can help. I have witnessed someone swollen up like an elephant, or getting bold during this time. Just go through it. Even if it was your choice it is heavy. If it was not the panic will be total. You might not be able to do your job anymore without her. She always was your right hand. There are a lot of things you cannot do anymore without him/her. Splitting up means the basis of your existence has fallen apart. In this time your claiming behaviour might reach the maximum. Stalking your ex, calling her up twenty times a day begging and blackmailing her to come home.

Another extreme way of cracking Pluto in the first house against your will, is when you find out everybody is afraid of you. Everybody is avoiding you. Nobody wants to do business anymore with you. Nobody explains. You don't understand how extremely violent you are. The louder you yell the more they put their back to you. The only thing left is to leave and start a new life abroad where no one has those bad memories of you. Your wife still loves you but her support does not go that far. She stays. You have to go by your own.

Cracking Pluto in the first house often means the end of the relationship. The last thing you should do, is to get another relationship right away to fill up the gap. If you do, the problem will only repeat itself on a worse scale. *It is necessary to live alone for a year or more to find out that you basically do not need a partner.* How come a man with three masters degrees and a high position can't fix his own meals and is so extremely lonely at night? Just go through it and learn it. If it comes down to it, you don't need anybody. That is how strong you are. Only in that position are you of real support. It takes at least a year to realise this truth deep from within. In that period you learn to love yourself. Once you have learned to be your own true self you are ready for a new relationship, a relationship in equality without dependence. You don't submit yourself anymore to the judgements of your partner. You do not need a partner to tell you how beautiful, strong and wise you are. More and more you act from your heart. You are not that tense anymore and your sex life will improve too, more balanced, less in a rush and more connected with your body.

Cracking Pluto doesn't always end in divorce. You can also work it out within your marriage. It begins with a self-consciousness: you do not want this stress anymore. If you have an escalating disagreement with your partner and your partner is blackmailing you to leave, you dare to say: "OK, leave then". If he doesn't, you will find your relationship has become more open. It means a new start. If your wife doesn't want to be your secretary anymore to do her own things accept it and find a solution ...... all by yourself.

Another way of cracking Pluto in the first house is as follows. Say, you are forty years old and you realise all the great things you have accomplished. A large queue of people admire you and are dependent on you. If you've got a problem just call him and it will be arranged. Why do you need more reassurance? You don't want it anymore. The next time they (your employer, your family, your spouse, your friends or whoever) approach you for your advice in their difficult times you say 'no'. First you are afraid they will turn against you. That's the 'who's side are you on' mentality. But if they are real friends they won't. Amazingly they don't turn against you. What a relief. A new start is made. Some kind of relaxation sets in.

Cracking Pluto is a continuous thing. You might temporarily fall back in your old habits again. For example with your children during transiting Pluto in the fifth house. They are not doing well and you want to help them or even worse: you feel ashamed for them. You've got the feeling they 'can't make it on their own'. You try to help them but you are projecting your own fears and frustrations onto them. You should keep on realising all those fears are your own fears.

When you have been through all this and you've cracked Pluto something has changed in your aura: you are more relaxed and you radiate a real self-confidence. In your work and social contacts, people will notice. You are much more open for critics and more free in your reactions. It will be much more easier to cooperate with you. You are not so defensive anymore. So on all sides the pearly gate will open, the horn of plenty.

Pluto in the second house

The drives and fears of Pluto in the second house are felt in the field of work, money, integrity and values. When you start a job you are doing the best you can. That is the drive. Together with this drive there is a basic fear of making mistakes. The slightest mistake can ruin your life totally. If the fears are bigger you are reluctant to start a job. You don't even start a project. Mysteriously you hang back. All that work ..... You get sick even thinking about it. All those traps you might step in .... You are making things more complicated than they are. Some have got a voice in their head telling them: "You dope! You jerk! You're never gonna be able to do that."

The past life calamities of Pluto in the second house revolve around work, difficult technical projects, money and the things you have done. Deep underneath you regret that you have made a bad mistake, an irreversible mistake in a past life. The consequences were terrible. People died, you died or other horrible things have happened because of your stupidity. In this life you are deadly afraid to make such a mistake again and you make sure you won't. Either you do nothing or you work like a dog.

I have recorded a big range of Pluto in the second house past life mistakes. It might be a silly mistake. For example you are standing on the wall of the duke's castle with his daughter in your arms. She makes an unexpected move and falls out of your arms on the wrong side of the wall forty feet down. Death. Your fault. Or you were a happy man with a loving wife and a newborn child and you decided to volunteer for the army not realizing you might get shot. Or you signed a wrong contract and your house was set in fire. Another story is a man who was an apprentice in the temple of Anubis. He got training in mummifying. The priests told him to do everything exactly as he had learned. But he thought: 'What do I care. Those bodies are dead anyway'. He was inaccurate, got infected and died of a terrible fever. A lot of natives with Pluto in the second house have had engineering jobs in past lives. The construction collapsed ..... Your fault. Most natives with Pluto in the second house were very integer in past lives. Despite of that, they got the blame and were hanged. Those are the ones who are born with a disgust and contempt for the lack of integrity of the common man. All those fools .... Steve Jobs was of this category. There is also a fear of corruption. In a past life you were a victim of corruption or you was caught being corrupted yourself. A lot of natives remember past lives of hard work and poverty. 'Boy have I been haying in that life.' They were proud of being a hard worker but at the end they were abused. They literally worked themselves to death for the work that never ends. With such a background you do nothing anymore in this life. You block when you have to do something. Past life poverties are often a reason for stress about money issues. You think you are not worthy to ask for so much money.

Children with Pluto in the second house have a drive to show how good they are. They are eager to learn. If you coach them well and give them the right stimulus they are able to perform greatly and they'll love it. But if they are neglected and nobody explains them how things are done they get upset. They need good coaching. Show them how things are done and don't emphasize their mistakes. Often they start things which are much too big and difficult for a little child and they fail. Their primary reaction is: run for your life and hide! Often the good things they do are not seen and the stupid things they do are highlighted, sneered at or punished. So if the negative reactions are too much they refuse to do anything anymore. They simply won't. They refuse to do their homework. They don't want to go to school anymore because the teacher is a fool. They go on strike mocking in a corner not being able to explain why they are so angry. The real reason is lack of recognition. You never do it right. Always there is something wrong. Often they have a stiff competition with an older brother or sister who is constantly outperforming them. Or, even worse, they are outperforming their older brother and he is constantly picking on you and putting you down. In school children with Pluto in the second house get stressed out when they have to perform. With their tongue out of their mouth they do the job in a moan. The teacher notices and thinks: 'Oh, he is having difficulties,' and he decides to give the child extra attention. That means: extra homework.

All children are good in some things and less in other things. Children with Pluto in the second house might develop a phobia for the things they are not good at. The teacher will notice and thinks: 'Oh, he is headstrong. I will give him extra exercises to make him learn'. A general pattern sets in, in which the child gets an extra training in the things he is not good at and never will be good at. The results might be hazardous. Either the child goes on strike or he develops skills which are not in line with his true qualities. In elementary school this is not so much a problem but later in high school and in college it is. They might wind up having a job they don't like. If you have a child with Pluto in the second house you should tell them: "Let somebody else do the things you are not good at and focus on the things you are good at." A lot of them will choose for an engineering profession.

When you have Pluto in the second house and your work is examined it often happens that you'll be treated unfairly. With an extra eye your work is watched. The teachers are standing in line with the red pencil. The moment you protest and you defend your point you get tensed and angry. This is considered as misbehavior. A rivalry between you and your teacher or your boss is created. You are put behind. You are rated inferior. You get a D for your work whereas someone else who has copied your work gets a B. With Pluto in the second house you will never forget that. A lot of natives with Pluto in the second house have a fear of exams. Exams evoke all kinds of stress and sleepless nights. So you are not fit during the test. But you have prepared yourself well and against all odds you still pass the test by one millimeter.

When people with Pluto in the second house have to do something they initially hesitate. 'Oh my god, what a work', they think. It takes a while before they start. But once they are started and the train is set in motion they can't stop anymore. They continue until they are exhausted. They don't feel like they are getting tired. Sometimes they start at the last moment and work non-stop for 24 hours to get the job done. This goes together with a lot of stress. Sometimes they are proud to perform that way. Proud to be a devil for work. Proud to be able to take on a lot of work with great precision and concentration. That is the Pluto in second house power. However an outsider would think: 'Why? Why are you making it so difficult? Wouldn't it be better if you would spread your activities in a more steady way?'

All natives with Pluto in the second house have their periods of being workaholic. They can't sleep thinking about all the things still must be done. 'Oh, I have to improve this or that. And don't forget to …..' Their work keeps on pursuing them. They also have periods of doing nothing when there is no motivation. But if there is a motivation they go. They can't sleep thinking of all the things they still have to do. There is a perfectionist's drive to perform better than great. They work on their list of procedures punctually and correctly. If they are put on a project they push through no matter how many setbacks. They do succeed but at the cost of a lot of stress. If they don't succeed and the project is cancelled it is a disaster and a psychiatrist is needed to clean up the mess in their soul.

Everyone with Pluto in the second house will experience a failed project at least once in their life. How frustrating. It is hard to talk about it without getting emotional. Who is to blame? The finger is pointed at you (just like in a past life) and you can't handle it. You literally get sick, knocked out. Natives with Pluto in the second house need a good supervisor in before cracking Pluto. There is a danger of being blind for the main lines and of focusing on the side lines. You are dug in by details. If so they might find you a rambler and you are.

Natives with Pluto in the second house experience a lot of stress at work. It is hard to see things in the right perspective. A lot of natives with Pluto in the second house have problems with their superiors. The communication is not right. Either you talk too much about your work or not at all. It might happen that your managers don't have any understanding about what you are doing. You have a lot of ideas but you forget to talk about them or you choose the wrong moment. Besides, your supervisor knows your working power and will exploit it. He is not there for your interest but for the interest of the company. He sets out the big lines and you execute the details. You are very good at that. But by sticking to executing jobs you never reach the top.

Natives with Pluto in the second house suffer a reluctance to promote themselves. You don't want to raise high expectations out of fear of not being able to follow through. You are critical. Above all you are critical of yourself. It seems like you are not satisfied with yourself because you want to outperform yourself. You are not a braggart. You explain how you could have done better. So you don't get the pay raise and you have to wait longer for a promotion. When you are asked to do the next job you don't dare to say: "Or I get a pay raise or I go." So you get stuck underpaid. You are gold without realizing it. You keep on fighting to climb up the ladder but as soon as the top is in reach you block. The switch from an executing job to a managers seat is a hard one.

At work natives with Pluto in the second house meet a lot of rivalry. You assume your colleagues share your integrity but they don't. They are jealous. They know you outperform them because you work under your level. They don't like that. You are always working and never having fun with your colleagues, not even at lunchtime. You miss the meeting because you were working. You get sabotaged. They saddle you with the most difficult and impossible targets. The moment you make a mistake they jump on you.

Another Pluto in the second house phenomenon is the self-made man. Someone who does everything by himself and delegates nothing to others. The only way to make sure the job is done well is by doing it yourself. They are persons of integrity and they hate the lack of integrity they see around them. They have got high values. They despise others who are not as sound as they are. Those are the Steve Jobs types.

Having an own company they start a project more complicated than they thought and they have to soldier on to avoid getting bankrupted. There are problems with asking the right price. Either you ask too much or too little. The moment it comes to pricing you block. There is a split in your attitude to money. First you are stressed by it and at the end of the negotiations you give it all out of your hands because suddenly you don't care anymore. When there is a billing issue they lose their clarity of mind holding themselves in so as not to explode. You overreact or do not react at all and the conditions are created to not get paid at all either because you did not react or because you are ashamed that you overreacted. Finally you decide: "Well, keep it then."

For natives with Pluto in the second house money is a big concern. They seem not to care but it controls their lives. They are nervous about it. They might run a multimillion dollar company while living themselves like a poor man with no luxury at all. They don't care for luxury. They only care for the project. Financial contracts are signed in fear and confusion. Afterwards they find out they signed a wrong contract. They need financial guidance. Before cracking Pluto there is no balance in this.

Some natives with Pluto in the second house go through the experience of being the victim of their own success. They start off with a very complicated project nobody believes in. In the beginning it is nothing but after years of struggling in the shade it suddenly becomes big. Your project catches the eye of financers, big companies and the media. Behind your back they are conspiring to take over your project. You are naïve because for you the work is the most important. You know nothing of all those intrigues because you were working. And then it happens: they are taking over your project. You are pushed aside. A team of well paid professionals take the lead and run away with the money. You get lured in, cheated and pushed out even by your own lawyer. What integrity? You thought your work was the most important but there were some other things you did not take into account. Only years later you realize what has happened. The split is: it was you who ran away. In the most difficult hour you went on your knees. You could not handle the tension. You lost yourself in the negotiations and you got mad.

When the fear is bigger than the drive you do nothing. You hesitate until it is too late. They panic when they have to apply for a job. At the end they wind up jobless living on welfare. They live in shabby homes on the wrong side of town not knowing what to do. The danger is not to fall into negativity and inertia. Keep on doing things although it is not for the money.

Some natives with Pluto in the second house have a stress about moral values. They try to reach the highest purity. The world is corrupted but they are not. They create their own lifestyle like an occult sect. They hate the money world. They do not want to participate in the capitalistic world. They withdraw in a barn growing their own crops, sew their own dresses and fix their own stuff. They endlessly recycle old trash. You might think: 'Oh, how cool.' But often it goes along with a lot of stress. For days, they are repairing that twenty year old washing machine. What a waste of time. They use second hand tools and they are making it harder on themselves than it should. Any argument about it makes them stressed out. The paradox is: they do not want to live by the common standard but they are not able to design a new coherent set of values either. Nobody understands them. They learn the art of living off nothing. They are not panicking when they don't have anything to eat anymore. They are panicking when they have smoked their last cigarette. They always survive because after all: a few days of vesting is not that bad. It is even healthy.

Every native with Pluto in the second house goes through a period where they are poor. Either they have to live on welfare or they save all their extra money for later. When they save money they do it in extremes: eating cat food to save money. Or they had a hard time when they were a student. Or they have a poverty problem after their bankruptcy. Or they were excommunicated for money reasons by their super rich family.

A silly feature of natives with Pluto in the second house is they can't throw old trash away. Their attic is full of old worthless stuff. When you throw something away it is gone. On the other hand they will make good collectors. It might happen that after 40 years this old classic computer you never threw away is worth a million!

During the cracking of Pluto natives with Pluto in the second house get in a crisis about their work. Are you really happy with your job? Are you reduced to a robot doing routine work? Pluto is transiting in the fifth house so your original and creative power is at stake. You simply cannot drag on doing dull routine jobs anymore. Or you have a creative scientific IT job but you are underpaid. During the cracking of Pluto a tremendous discontent takes over. Somehow you got stuck in your work. Something must change.

Sometimes the change is brought on by the circumstances. Somehow you find yourself in a position to renegotiate your job conditions. It comes to the point where you slap your fist on the table and demand a high rank and a high salary. You put your cards on the table about what kind of work you want to do. You have done so many projects and they know your integrity. You have always been gold for the company and you are ready for a big promotion. If not ……. Two things might happen. Or they go for it, or not. If they do, you won the battle and you cracked Pluto.

If they don't you have to go. Cracking Pluto in the second house often means you get thrown out of your financial securities. Cracking Pluto in the second house means to not panic over financial setbacks. Don't be a slave for a few bucks. When you go and choose for financial insecurity at least you are not stuck with a job you don't like. Although you think it is the end of the world it gives you a new start. You are able to choose again. You have to go through all this stress as a karmic release. Often you start a new profession adding to what are you already can do. It could be you are of the category of the ones who learned a profession not matching your true qualities. Deep in your heart you definitely know what you want. But you never dared because of the money. You take the heavy decision: 'I won't work for Maggie's farm no more and I will make my hobby my profession. I trust in the Providence that I will not starve the death.' You jump and you make your hobby your profession. You combine making money with joy. Initially it will be very scary but persistent as you are you'll manage. There is no greater joy than doing the things you love. The trick is to stay cool in the negotiations. Be patient in pulling the rope. Don't get upset when things don't go easy.

Cracking Pluto in the second house means the end of

your stress at work. It is the end of being afraid of making mistakes. Reviewing your life you conclude: "I have made many mistakes in my life and I know I will make many more. That's life". Indeed, that is life and that is the relief. From now on your work will be lighter. No more rush or hurry. No panic by setbacks. Making mistakes is part of humanity. You'll become a much nicer person to cooperate with. All rivalry is gone. The conditions are created to enter the management field and to leave the executing job behind. No more irritation when someone jerks off. Everything you touch change into gold calm and easy. You learn to spread your activities better. Although it is about big money, with a smile you explain to them what to do. Amazing how easy it is. It feels like parasitizing but it is not. You concentrate on the main lines and leave the details to others. If you can't and you keep on nagging about the details and controlling the nitwits you fail like Steve Jobs. He died a Plutonic death. He never enjoyed the fruits of his enterprise. Eventually he collapsed from his own irritation.

On the spiritual plane cracking Pluto in the second house means you will be less judgmental. No despise anymore for people less precise than you. No stress anymore in dealing with values. You made your mistakes let someone else make theirs.
Cracking Pluto in the second house is to learn to enjoy the fruits of your productivity. Initially that will be hard because deep inside you are a buzzy bee. Drinking cocktails on a palm beach doing nothing is not a lasting option. You would get bored. There is always something to do. After cracking Pluto the main reason for your activities will be whether you like it or not. Does it fit in your values? Does it raise your enthusiasm? By your enthusiasm all you

touch changes into gold.

Pluto in the third house

Pluto in the third house means a tension in communicating, a stress in what you should say and what you really think. You want a profound contact but you don't dare to show yourself. You are afraid to say something wrong. The slightest wrong statement and it is over. So you stay superficial to avoid being pinned down on an opinion. When the fear is bigger than the drive you stay quiet and you let the other do the talking. Let him make the wrong statements. When your drive to communicate is bigger than your fear you are very talkative but you don't really say anything. The moment you feel a deeper contact you get scared and you hold off. Natives with Pluto in the third house experience a lot of loneliness. The moment somebody comes too close they get overwhelmed by emotions 'too big to handle'. They feel isolated from their pals. There is a wall in between. Unconsciously they sustain their own isolation. To be frank: the wall is theirs.

The fear of true contact originates in past lives when intrigues, lies or a total lack of communication ruined your life. You were cheated. Deep in your heart you don't trust anyone. "Also you, Brutus?", Ceasar spoke when he was stabbed in his back by his trustee.
There is a big variety of past life experiences causing a fear to speak out truly. Either you were naïve. One slip of the tongue and your best friend was killed. If you kept quiet it would not have happened ...... Or you were a wise man and the best friend and first advisor of the king. For years you were together daily. One day the king says something

and you know it is not true. You ask him why he is lying that way. Next you were thrown in jail and your tongue is cut out. Or you were a general and you had perfect contact with another general. Together you won all the wars. One day an argument rose. That same moment you were stabbed to death.

Another Pluto in the third house calamity is when something was not communicated well. If there had been some more talking it would not have happened. The decision was made behind your back. In this life you listen once, twice and again to make sure you understand. When you disagree you don't say it. Or you failed to have real contact no matter how you tried. After years of talking you gave up trying and did not argue anymore because they won't understand anyway. In this life you are born with the same desperate feeling the moment you talk to someone. They won't understand anyway. You know what it is all about but you don't dare to say.

Sometimes the Pluto in the third house past lives pain is just a regret about being superficial. You were a drunk only making fun and running away from the real things of life. Or you were a brainwashed soldier. Or you were isolated and locked up at home. You were the stupid one. Now in this life you don't dare to say anything substantial out of fear of being superficial.

With Pluto in the third house you feel socially handicapped with your friends, your partner, your colleagues and everyone you meet. Especially dealing with important people is an agony: the ones you are dependent on, the ones you admire. The split is: You expect to get something beautiful in contacting but you hold back and as a result you get nothing.

Little children with Pluto in the third house tell you hundreds of stories even when they are not able to talk yet. In those early years they have their own language. Being together they want your full attention. When you don't listen well they get mad. Having a child with Pluto in the third house it might be very exhausting to talk with. They talk fast so you need all your concentration to follow their deep thinking. They notice immediately when you are absent-minded and get emotionally upset by your superficiality. This might happen daily or once in a while. Finally they give up talking about themselves.

Children with Pluto in the third house are very spontaneous, expressive and curious. When you meet a child with Pluto in the third house they unpack all your pockets to see what is in there, your wallet, your credit cards, your notebooks and all your personal things. They want to share everything and get extremely excited. As a reaction they are stopped. People might feel uneasy with all that curiosity. The excitement of a child with Pluto in the third house when meeting is sheer power. The power is too big to handle and is put through the mill. The finger is raised: 'don't be silly, don't do that and don't say that. Be normal'. Their hunger for true contact is not seen. The child meets incomprehensible reactions. A fear sets in and they start holding in their spontaneity. They develop all kinds of meeting rituals. First they pretend not to notice. Later, after an outflanking movement they do their greetings. The older they get the more they wait to see which way the wind blows. At the end they don't react at all.

Pluto in the third house fears roughly work out in one or two ways. Either you always keep your mouth shut as a mouse or you are a chatterbox talking for hours about nothing. The silent types don't say anything for safety reasons. You know, words will hang you. When you don't say anything you don't say anything wrong either. So you let the other do the talking. That is much easier. For days they can be locked up in their silence not being able to get one word out of their throat. Natives with Pluto in the third house are good listeners. They are very keen on whether you are true and consistent with what you say. If it is not they won't say a thing. They avoid an argument. 'Ugh, stranger speaks with double tongue', they think and they turn their back locking themselves up in their loneliness. They don't dare to speak out the truth and they also don't dare to lie. Sometimes the tension is heard in their voice. As though they first have to push before you talk.

The talkative ones talk endlessly as long as it has nothing to do with themselves. They know all the gossips and pass it along. Nothing is more fun than to blow off steam in a superficial flood of words.. They talk about how well they know things. They talk about other people like they are common good. That can be very funny. Sometimes they are good entertainers. They talk about everything ….. but themselves. They will ask your opinion without giving their own. Since it is very hard to be true and consistent they don't try. They make sure what they say is in line with the common good. They joke a lot out of fear of being taken seriously. They can be really funny and razor blade sharp but when it gets too personal they quickly change the topic. They are masters in diversionary tactics in their efforts to avoid being put in an awkward position.

The power of Pluto in the third house is the magic of meeting. There is a curiosity, a need to meet people. Your perception is superb and your remarks, if spoken out frankly, are right.

For the talkative ones making the first contact is not the

problem. Often they have got a standard strategy to make the first contact. Carefully they make sure not to step on toes. They are good at public relations affairs. But it is formal. The problem is personal contact. With Pluto in the third house the first contact evokes big emotions, good or bad. Those emotions are not wanted and are hidden. When you dislike someone you are afraid it is seen. When you like somebody you are afraid to get cheated. In the communication those issues are avoided.

For the silent types the magic in meeting is too big to handle. You are afraid of the encounter. Having important meetings is an agony. It is so important to make a good impression. The agony is you have to say something but you get nervous and you don't know what you say anymore. Suddenly you suffer the incomprehensible disease of having a paralyzed tongue. This strikes you very physically. It is like fainting. As a result the meeting becomes a disaster. You do not dare to speak about what you want. You don't come to the point. The power of Pluto in the third house is the analysis. Your analysis is razor sharp, killing. It might cause even sharper reactions. So you hold back on it smothering all spontaneity. How to tell the bad message? Don't shoot the messenger. You are afraid for the confrontation and you keep your mouth shut. Natives with Pluto in the third house experience a lot of loneliness and isolation.

In the end the Pluto in the third house problem is an emotional problem. To avoid those emotions you stay formal. Don't hurt others. Don't get hurt. There is a lot you perceive you don't talk about. That is too direct. You keep the contact mental. It is about the content of words. Is it right what you say? You study a lot to be sure you won't get cornered in. You prepare yourself to have an answer on every naughty question you might get. You stay within the codes. At school and within your profession this is a mighty tool for a successful career. But as you go on you'll find out you get locked up in formalities. You easily handle every business case sitting the whole day in an office doing nothing. As a manager you make sure to be everybody's friend. You don't show yourself. You are colourless no matter how casual you try to behave. With Pluto in the third house you don't easily admit that you have a problem. Imagine what happens when you admit. You will be asked to explain yourself. You get sick by the mere thought. So, everything is cool and fine.

Holding back on your communication abilities basically means holding back on love energies. Giving that blink of love creates all kinds of expectations you are afraid of. Is it safe to give that blink or will it be used against me? Still you do have your preferences. When you fall in love it is hard to show. Nobody notices how deeply the meeting is felt because of the blank expression on your face. All kind of pretences are used to not get to the point. You might even fall in love with someone at work and for years nobody knows.

The isolation of natives with Pluto in the third house is also felt in marriage. You let the other do the proposals and the talking. So you get overruled. You hand over your power of speech. You hide behind a ninth house pretence of how you should be. However within a marriage it is harder to hide. So it is more likely to fall out of your defensive role when you can't hold back anymore. Hopefully your spouse will understand and come closer to you that way.

The isolation of Pluto in the third house comes to a maximum when transit Pluto squares natal Pluto and you will be challenged to break out. Either you can't bear your isolation anymore and you crawl out yourself or you get in problems because your formal attitude is not accepted anymore.

Mostly the cracking of Pluto in the third house starts in your job when transiting Pluto crosses the sixth house. Your colleagues want you to speak out. They want you to be clear, to show your colour and to take sides. On that moment you are scared the death. You started your career at the bottom. As a little man it was a wise policy to keep your mouth shut and do the best you could. But now after all your promotions you are expected to show leadership. Your employees want you to be open and shine your light. They get insecure if you constantly hide yourself in formalities. They want to see your real face. They want to know where they are at with you. They want leadership. And that is the problem. To put it frankly: you can't. Excuse me: you can but you don't dare. As long as you don't show your colour the calamity is pending. Your employees go on strike because they don't know about your intentions. They are figuring up the wildest rumours. Intrigues are spawned, exactly what you don't want. They might consider you a twister. You always sit on the fence. The same counts for your business associates. It might happen that an important project is cancelled because of your lack of clarity. You did not dare to cut the knot. Or worst a project fails because your associate packs his bags. He finally doubted your commitment. He did not know anymore where he was at with you. Coping with all those problems, no matter you if manage to talk yourself out of it or not, you will understand all this would not have happened if you were more open and clear about yourself from the beginning. Once you realise this you make a firm decision to be more open in the future and you crack Pluto. Now that you are a man of decision you should show leadership with a personal touch. What you should do is to speak out clearly just as it is. Stay diplomatic but be clear. No matter if you die all deaths, just do it and you'll win. If it comes to the climax you say a super prayer, you send the final e-mail releasing your true opinion. You go to the meeting and you tell them what you want and where you stand. You see you will win. And if it means you have to pack your bags, just do it and find your luck somewhere else.

If you never got a high rank the same thing happens. No matter how, the moment comes when you are summoned to declare yourself. During the period of cracking Pluto your superiors want to know where you are at. For years you have been working obediently as an anonymous and now they want to know about your ambitions. They want to know who you are. You are invited to the headquarters and you have to speak out. At that moment you have to crack Pluto. If you block, you blow it and you'll regret it for the rest of your life. I remember a clerk in a library. She was invited to the central office to talk about her career. On the way she turned back home feeling puking sick and miserable. Cracking Pluto in the third house is to go to that important meeting, die all deaths, and simply explain yourself, easy and relaxed. The problem is only in your head.

With Pluto in the third house you will be forced to speak out. It might be there are some things you don't accept anymore. You have to speak out. For example your boss wants you to do a project you don't like. Or your spouse is cornering you in too much. You have to speak out clearly and finally you get what you want or you stay in a situation you don't want. Cracking Pluto in the third house is putting your cards on the table. That is a holy duty. It feels like dying. 'They will never get along with it,' you think. The scary thing is: will you stand firm or not. If you don't you will get another chance to crack Pluto later. If you do and you manage to make yourself clear you are released from the pressure. A big transformation has taken place. You are taken seriously. If it does mean the end it is at least the end of a living hell. You'll try your fortunes somewhere else. Now that you have spoken out you became also clear for yourself and you'll be consistent with it. You have grown because now you know yourself better about what you accept or not and have learned to open your mouth.

Cracking Pluto in the third house means a transformation in your personal contacts. You might find out you don't have any friends. You become more intimate. In business but also in your marriage and social contacts in general. You might realise your marriage is stranded in mutual isolation. All communication has stopped and there is nothing between you two anymore. Either you make a new start or it is the end. There is an obligation to talk. Your spouse already gave it up. It might be you fall in love with somebody who mysteriously opens you up. Just admit the truth and speak out. Talk about it and take the consequences. Suppose you are one of the silent types and you never dared to start a love affair. When you fall in love during this transit you are confronted with a 'now or never' situation. If you blow it this time you can forget it for the rest of your life. This compulsion gives you wings. In this period you are in the fidgets. But without this compulsion you never would have opened up. And to your surprise it works out alright. What a relief.
Or you have been in love for years with your manager but he is not. You never showed it and he is unaware. Besides he is married and he would not think about an affair. You

only suffer. During cracking Pluto you realise your isolation and you break out and leave the company.

Cracking Pluto in the third house also might concern solving problems with your neighbours. Your neighbours are incessantly harassing you. You stay formal and decent but you don't know what to say or do. They keep on intimidating, accusing and provoking you. Since you don't dare to give them a peace of your big mouth they get nastier and nastier. During cracking Pluto you break out. You tell everybody about their nasty games. Everybody in the neighbourhood, the police, your lawyer, your therapist and the mayor himself. This communication is your weapon and they will stop their evil ways. Some say: "You must thank your neighbours for opening you up." But I don't believe that. They should not be nasty.

Cracking Pluto in the third house you have to show your colour. With transiting Pluto in the fifth house it is about to show your creative ideas and to be completely open with your children. With transiting Pluto in the sixth house it turns around taking responsibility in your job and with transiting Pluto in the seventh house it is to be completely honest and open with your partner.

Cracking Pluto in the third house primarily means honesty to yourself and about your own emotions. You throw away your breathtaking fear for conflicts. In the beginning it might be overwhelming for your colleagues, spouse and everyone you deal with. But they get used to it. The power of Pluto in the third house is the ability to listen, to analyse and finally to explain. That is the winning option.

During cracking Pluto in the third house you crawl out of your shell of self-defence and a relaxation in contacting people sets in. It becomes your joy. Your communication powers burst open. You lose your passivity. You say exactly what it is about. You don't wait until you are asked something. Out of commitment you'll be the first to tell. In the right moment the right remark and the right gesture and the miracle is done. By your own directness doors will be opened which would have stayed closed for you otherwise. It is fascinating to talk with you because you talks profoundly and straight from your heart. During your life you have been mainly observing. You built up a lot of knowledge and insight. Now you speak up and your arguments and considerations are overwhelming. They all go for it. In your job and in general this all will be to your advantage. What once was your weakness now becomes your power. You have got to show your colour and your light. Once you were formal and distant, now you have regained your directness. Your popularity only grows when you curse when something unexpected happens. You are powerful enough not to get hanged for one wrong word.

The power of Pluto in the third house is the ability to build bridges between people. By your openness you create a bond of commitment you always longed for. During cracking Pluto in the third house you get back your spontaneity and warm-heartedness. If all goes well you have a myriad of contacts. In the communication you touch the deeper layers of life. It means harvesting the fruit of life, the horn of plenty.

Pluto in the fourth house

Pluto in the fourth house bares a feeling of being under-estimated. You have got a fear of being not good enough. You feel like you are treated like a nobody and you want to scream out you are not something less.

The split of Pluto in the fourth house is that you long for a warm nest but it is never good enough. You suffer a love/hate relationship with your family. Always there is something wrong in family affairs. It starts with the family you are born in. Your parents don't see who you really are. Their realm is different from yours. With Pluto in the fourth house there always is something wrong with the social class you are born in. Either they are from poor social class or they are snobbish, bourgeois or something else. You do want to cooperate since you long for a harmonious family life but …... It is hard to submit to the family rules. As a grown up you suffer an ambiguity towards marriage. You want to marry but when you do you feel miserable in it. After the divorce living alone is miserable too so you marry again to experience the same dissatisfaction in your next marriage. A lot of natives with Pluto in the fourth house marry and divorce several times in their life.

With Pluto in the fourth house you have got nasty past life memories in family affairs. You were deeply humiliated. Your soul has been hurt in its self-esteem. In a past life you have suffered total repression in your marriage. Your spouse was putting you down to the maximum until you believed yourself you were worthless. For example: you did not produce children and for that you were worthless.

Sometimes it went together with gross intimidation and violence. Although your husband always threatened you to kill you, you never believed he would do it too. And then …… he did it too. As a result you are struggling in this life for your self-respect. Sometimes the Pluto resentment is a general hate against the class society. In past lives you were born as a beggar and you remained a beggar. There was no way out. In this life you again are born in a socially deprived family. Deep in your unconsciousness you want to shout out: "I do not belong to those people. I am made of gold." In rare cases you were a tyrant yourself. As a despot nobody could come close to you and you became unhappy, cruel and unfair. You were annoyed with everything and everybody. You hated life for no reason and above all you hated yourself. You lost your roots, the connection with yourself. After cracking Pluto this n is restored. I also recorded a Pluto in the fourth house past life of somebody who lost all her family and tribe in a big earthquake followed by a giant tsunami. She was the sole survivor and died right after out of sadness. Her family was dear to her. When she was thirty she had her third husband.

A child with Pluto in the fourth house does not feel at ease at home. There is always a reason to dig in your heels. It comes to clashes and the child loses. They have a different mind. For example the child is very artistic and creative and the parents are very strait and formal. Or the parents are sloppy and the child is very neat and precise. The parents are of poor education and the child is very intelligent. Despite your spiritual and philosophical mind you were raised in the ghetto. Or you were born and raised in a middle of nowhere town in the midlands with no culture or style. The child feels he is forced to participate in family affairs. Somehow the family affairs are very demanding.

Every weekend the whole family has to join in the same. For example they all go to the sports club and the child has to join although he is not sportive at all. Or they all have to help in the family company. I recorded a case of a very sensitive healer, a magnetizer, whose father was a butcher with his own slaughterhouse. Every weekend he and the whole family had to help finishing the deboning job. He hated it but had to. He became vegetarian. He hated his father and he was ashamed of having such a background. Nobody ought to know. Everybody knew. Another case is a woman whose mother was a psychoanalyst. Everything she said and did was scrutinized followed by an advice how to get along next time. She never agreed but could not win the argument. Later she became very dependent because she did not dare to make decisions by herself.

When children with Pluto in the fourth house notice they are not understood a superpower is activated and the child explodes. The child wants credit for his own likings. By family law he has no say over his own activities. He explodes but that does not make it any better, on the contrary. The child holds in its disgust and becomes obedient. The resistance becomes passive. Their blood is boiling but they shut up. If the fear is bigger the parents only find out later the child did not like it. If the drive is bigger the child becomes antisocial. He hides himself in his own room. The child is troublesome. Quite often the parents really do not understand what is wrong. The child does not understand it either. He cannot explain it. Both parents and child long for good family relations but it does not work out. It is incomprehensible. Pluto fears are irrational. It is not that easy to raise a child with Pluto in the fourth house. They can hurt you deeply by their rejection.

With Pluto in the fourth house you are ashamed for your

background. You look down on your family. You longed for education and culture but you did not get any support. Against all odds you worked yourself up. In the end you have got all masters degrees and you raised above your family class. However, you still have got their accent revealing your low background giving you a disadvantage. You are ashamed for your accent and your simple parents. You are hurt being raised in a boring small isolated town filled with retards. However your parents, although not that intelligent, are very sweet and loving. They even adore you. But to you they are dumb apes and you cannot hide your irritation. Why are you so cold?

At school the same problem of feeling misunderstood and underestimated will be triggered too. When the child does not get the credit he deserves the feeling of being a nobody pops up again. At school the child hides his anxiety. But when he comes home he throws his school bag in the corner and grudges and cries. As a parent you might feel sorry for the unhappiness of your child. When you try to talk it out your child might not always be that reasonable. He accepts no advice. There is no advice. However your child does need you. At home the steam is blown off. If it is possible to talk about it, no matter how floundering, the frustration is worked out and the child will be able to start the next day with a good spirit. But in most cases that does not happen and the child stands alone.

Later in life natives with Pluto in the fourth house find their Waterloo in their marriage. It is a common pattern to start a marriage with high expectations to be dramatically disappointed later on. There is a drive to create an ideal family-life. A tension is built up when they find themselves unable to do so. It is even more wicked. I have heard stories (not only one) of natives with Pluto in the fourth house who realized during the wedding they actually did not want to. They did not dare to say 'no'. They had to. Within a year the divorce was settled leaving her husband upset, desperate and jealous.

If the fear is bigger than the drive you blame yourself. Especially women have a tendency to blame themselves. They do their utter best to be a perfect housewife. But it is overdone. Every time when a problem occurs they overreact. Time and again you sense something is wrong without being able to touch the essence. It is not understood or taken seriously. You are running around and negotiating your guts off like a slave to solve all family problems and he seems not to care. In fact you are the problem. You make an Elephant out of a mouse. He does not recognize 'the problem' being so big. Of course not. He even might get irritated. Next you feel to blame for his irritation. Being married is a desperate thing for natives with Pluto in the fourth house. It means dying a thousand deaths. You suffer terrible uncertainties. You are looping the problems to the desperation of your family. An outsider would say: "Family problems have always existed right from the beginning of mankind. So what are you so upset about." By the time of cracking Pluto you either realize how you always overreacted and the situation will ease up. Or you get a divorce (kicked out) leaving you with the feeling 'what the hell did I do wrong?'.

If the drive is bigger than the fear your partner is to blame. It is always his or her fault. You fall in love, start a family life and after a while you find out your partner does not understand you. First you were not understood by your parents and now you are not understood by your partner.

You talk and talk with no result. An enormous discontent sets in. You expect your partner to do his best too but he does not. As a woman you find your partner a nobody and he is to blame for all the miseries in your marriage. My man is not a man. He is a weak ass. As a man you find your wife simply not good enough. You become antisocial looking out for someone else. When you have found someone else you divorce. You arrange your next marriage before divorcing. Somehow for natives with Pluto in the fourth house living alone is not an option. Such a situation is not wanted. Being single is a rare exception. It will be remembered as bad times.

A lot of men with Pluto in the fourth house set all their goals on a career. They hide themselves behind their work. They go for their reputation (tenth house) and their private life is side issue. They walk away from their parenting job. You leave it to your wife. As a silent contract he makes the money and his wife takes care for the rest, the laundry and the good harmony in the family. Often he is married with someone from his own social class he despises so much. He doesn't divorce. That is not done. By the time of cracking Pluto he realizes his discontent and divorces. Immediately he is remarried. This time with a woman from a higher social class. But behold, there is a viper in the grass, getting problems with his new family in law. Now that he is part of the upper class everybody will know it too. He always knows better thanks to his high education. He will be sneered at. Why does he need all this self-glorification? Is there something wrong with his self-esteem? No matter how important he tries to be the family in law finds him a scoundrel. They see through his image building. So he has to crack Pluto again to learn modesty.
Some women with Pluto in the fourth house choose for

a career instead of raising children. They rise up high in business being an advocate of not having children. The moment transit Pluto squares the natal Pluto they get a mysterious longing for a child. Your basic instincts beat your intellectual considerations. You realize it might be too late if you wait longer. Deep from your unconsciousness a wish pops up to raise a child. You crack all your reserves with family affairs and get that child. Once I had a reading with a woman being a big shot in a multinational food company. She was thirty six. She was single. She asked me where she would be the happiest. In Hong Kong, Monaco or should she stay in Amsterdam? I told her she would get pregnant and should accept her husband unconditionally. She got furious. "NEVÉÉÉR, NEVÉÉÉR, NEVÉÉÉR", she yelled.

Having children is for most natives with Pluto in the fourth house troublesome or at least ambiguous. Often children are considered a burden. Children cost money. Children are cute but they are a millstone on your back.
Suppose you are a man working yourself up on the social ladder. You don't divorce because that is too troublesome and not good for your reputation. You find your wife not good enough and neither your child. Your child does not meet your expectations. Your child is just as dumb as your wife. As a result your child gets troublesome flunking out of school and misbehaving himself. And then, when your wife tells you she is pregnant for a second time you divorce.
Especially women with Pluto in the fourth house are ambiguous towards children. If they get children at a young age it is 'a mistake'. Left by their partner they are stuck with a child. An extreme emotional love/hate relationship between mother and child sets in. They feel they need a man

to help raising the child but the child itself is a hindrance to find a new man. At least that is what they think. They cannot get out to find a man because they have to stay home stuck with their child. Marrying her is also marrying her child. The split is: the child is to blame for it and still she has to love and care for him.

Even if having a child was not a mistake woman with Pluto in the fourth house find raising children extremely difficult. They feel a lot of uncertainty. They doubt doing the right thing. If the child has a problem they overreact. In some cases they are perfect mothers not realizing it. In other cases they are too critical wanting the child to live up to their expectations. Raising a child is not that easy especially not for someone with Pluto in the fourth house.

With Pluto in the fourth house you desperately want a happy family. But it is never good enough. If you marry before the cracking of Pluto a potential bomb is hidden under the carpet. You need a partner to saturate your family life with love, protection and understanding. In rare cases you find such a partner. Such an ideal person does not exists. The answer for this problem begins with realizing the problem is in you. The discontent is in you. The moment you realize this all ice will melt and the sun will shine again. In general this is easier to realize for women than for men. Men are more stubborn. Often there is a form of overestimation. They project their minority feelings in haughtiness. An 'I am always right' attitude sets in.

Cracking Pluto in the fourth house concerns your spouse, your 'best' friend. Transit Pluto goes through the seventh house, the house of relationships. Before the cracking you were not able to name your discontent. You were doing your duty trying to structure your marriage (transit Pluto in the sixth house). You did your best but ….. You tried to alter the structure by divorcing and marrying another. Or you stayed married not realizing you had already given up all hopes. Now transit Pluto enters the seventh house you begin to realize. The situation comes to a climax. It can't last any longer. By the cracking of Pluto the bomb under the carpet of your marriage explodes. You decide to solve the problem once and for all. Either you divorce or you save your marriage miraculously.

Your marriage might be saved by talking and by introspection with or without the help of a therapist. Your eyes are opened and you find out your spouse and your children love you very much. From then on you decide to make the best you can of your family life and accept the differences. No more nagging when a problem occurs but stay calm, talk it out and have confidence. However in this process you need a spouse who understands. Suppose deep in your heart you always blamed your husband but never told him. Now that you tell you realize he was just as desperate as you for all those misunderstandings. After all it was all in yourself.

A man with Pluto in the fourth house putting all emphasis on work and neglecting his family might suddenly be left alone. Blind as he was he did not foresee it. Suddenly he has to bake his own eggs. His wife won't come back. This way he gets a shock therapy and in his next marriage he makes sure he pays enough attention to his wife.

In general cracking Pluto in the fourth house means a draw back from career and reputation stress and a come back to your private life and the ones you love. The cosmos will force you to go back to your roots. After a deep self-inquiry about the origin of your discontent you get even with your parents. You find a way to handle them and go your own way at the same time. Doing this inner journey it would be a good thing to write it down or to find a therapist/counsellor to join this journey to find out who you really are and what you really want. You find peace with yourself. Once you have rediscovered your true psychic power you will choose to put in all your energies for the well-being of your (new) family. In return you get the horn of plenty.

Cracking Pluto in the fourth house means creating a family. In almost all cases it means some kind of marriage or oath. Your next relation will be completely different. From the lessons learned you will make sure it will work out this time. That is a karmic goal. However I did meet people who were happy living alone after four divorces. Their family is the cosmos. Their marriage is spiritual, not bounded by one a person. It is all based on self-acceptance. Once you've made the jump and have gone through all your fears of being not good enough you also grow in power on other fields. It all becomes warmer and easier.

Pluto in the fifth house

Pluto in the fifth house gives a drive and a fear to be the center of attention. There is a drive to be a star. But the moment you rise up and everyone is watching you, you get scared and you hide. So you don't. This means you restrict yourself on your creative life force. You have a great imagination, that is the power, but you are reluctant to show it. It is like you have too many ideas and don't know which ones to choose. So you hold back on your spontaneity. You don't dare to let yourself go. Doing the things you love is not allowed. You get tensed up when you are supposed to be free and informal.

The fear comes down to being wanted too much. Somewhere in a past life a calamity occurred during parties. You got caught because you were so special and (sexually) attractive. Being the dancing queen of the blasting royal party you were kidnapped because of your beauty and the riches of your family. You were terribly abused and raped. A fear is created that it will happen again when you totally let yourself go. Or the party happened to be the climax of a political (eleventh house) plot. Fighting broke out with deadly results all about you. Or during the party you were lured in with beautiful promises but they only wanted to control you, winding up in sadism. In those past life experiences you concluded always to be alert and to not let yourself go.
A lot of times there are past life memories of unhappy lives because having fun was not allowed. You lived in a celibate condition, in a serious atmosphere. You were locked up in

a monastery without fun and laughter. Indulging in human frivolities and especially love was bad, even a deadly sin. You were cut off from social contacts. You were married with no sex or love from the beginning. In those cases you have a drive to get what you missed in your past life: be the clown, love your sex-life and show off your beauty. But you don't dare because it is programmed into your soul that is a bad thing. Being born with Pluto in the fifth house means you are meant to get rid of this programming. That is the drive.

The Pluto in the fifth house archetype is: you were happy in an ancient paradise and suddenly you were bitten by a snake. You died in a high fever wondering what went wrong. In this life you watch out not to walk naively in (the devil's) paradise and you stay alert. On the field of creative ideas it might be you were in a past life an insane professor doing much harm with his wicked inventions like doctor Strangelove. You were proud of being such a genius all by egoism. After your death you felt a deep regret.

Children with Pluto in the fifth house are very active. They live out their creative energy in all its spontaneity. The child needs a lot of attention. He expects you to share his creative world. He makes a lot of noise. His energy is too much. A parent needs a break too. A stop is put to his energies. "Be quiet. Behave. Don't do that. Are you crazy?" He finds out people get mad when he is loud. That's not what he wants. He gets canned in. He is told to get his hands off. Sometimes his parents are dull. The parents simply can't follow the child. He is too fast. Or the parents are very strict in what is allowed and what is not. He has got to be neat. No child likes to be put in a box but a child with Pluto in the fifth house will try to escape with all its might. Maybe the first break outs will be won but eventually it will be in vain. The box will be reconstructed until no escape is possible anymore. In the end the child promises itself to hold in its energies. Think first! He gets blocked in his spontaneity. Not only the family puts a block on his energies, nature does too. Playing wildly the toys get damaged. So he decides for himself to be more careful. Or he gets in a fight. When he realizes afterwards what has happened he decides never ever to lose control again. Nothing at hand because children don't fight deadly. But the child is panicking. Even a push of a girlfriend might become a drama. A past life fear is triggered. As a parent you should explain them it is not that bad. It happens a lot that a friendship with a Pluto in the fifth house persons ends because of a silly scrimmage.

No matter how, the spontaneity of a child with Pluto in the fifth house will be restrained. Also at school a fear is triggered. In school you should shut up and pay attention to what the teacher says. Being loud and wild will get you into problems for lack of discipline. The child makes a promise to be alert under all circumstances and to think twice before acting. The message is: adapt to the situation and don't be the central figure. Don't make such a ruckus. If you do so, the worst things will happen. A fear is triggered. His behavior pattern becomes a protocol. The child becomes a good girl/guy like it ought to be. Physically they look relaxed. Nobody notices their tension. Sure their creative hyper energy is still there. The tension is in their head. From a distance natives with Pluto in the fifth house are very boring people. But they don't care. They are even proud of it. Rather boring than being crucified. When you know them better you will find out they have a very vivid mind. They have all kinds of ideas they don't dare to bring into practice. Talking on a one-to-one basis they dare to express their ideas but if more people get involved or when they are in a group they become quiet. They distrust their own ideas and they fear the public reaction.

When going out to parties a native with Pluto in the fifth house will react in one or two ways:
1) If the fear is bigger than the drive they will detest parties. They don't feel at ease at parties. They will only go to parties as an obligation. Parties are too wild. That is scary. They would rather do something useful. The moment they are supposed to get their ya ya's out and have fun they get anxious. They fear parties and sex. The boys become the boring nerds and the girls become prudish, prim and proper goats.
2) If the drive is bigger than the fear they don't skip a single party. They go with the latest hype. It all happens downtown in the dancing halls and the meeting places. That's where the action is. Downtown ….. In some cases their entire life all turns about sex. You know: sex is very important.

The party trippers don't go to parties to get their rocks off. It's their work. They won't dance themselves. They stay in the background. They keep track of everything that happens. Their conversation is serious. They are doing business. Pretty soon they become a member of the crew. They get a job in the show business, in the advertisement world, on cruise ships or they organize holiday trips. Everything having to do with the world of glamour and glitter. They organize it. There is no business like show business. They are not the star themselves. They organize DJ competitions to choose the star. They are not the attraction themselves although they dream of being one. They are part of the crew, staying in the background making sure, being alert, everything goes well. They are very trendy in a creative world but are holding back on their own true creativity. If the drive is mighty big they become a model. You'll be surprised how many models have Pluto in the fifth house. It is a very lonely business to be constantly on roadshows staying in hotels in unknown towns. Not good for a stable love life. But somehow it is their karmic lot to be in the spotlight without being shot. On the other hand: A lot of natives with Pluto in the fifth house unconsciously dream of being a top model but they don't dare. They don't even try.

The nerds detesting parties suffer past lives of fears that things would get out of hand. The moment the situation gets informal and loose a feeling of danger sets in. Now that it is celebration time, it does not mean that everything is allowed! The worst thing is when you suddenly become the center of all the attention. When you win a prize or something like that. You'll be panicking.

Natives with Pluto in the fifth house have a remarkable blank expression on their face. You can't read anything from it. Behind that poker face a high intensity engine is running fast. In a split second all the consequences and conclusions that might be drawn are thought of. It happens automatically. You can't see it. On the outside they look completely calm but in the inside a high speed brain engine is rotating.

A lot of natives with Pluto in the fifth house are good scientists. Somehow they know how to make the dullest issues interesting as long they can project their creative and analytic mind on it. Technical issues, law, administrative solutions, chess and philosophic issues as long they can sit on their chair. Other people would fall asleep but they push through. At work they might come with surprising ideas. When they have an original idea they are brooding on it for a long time. Before cracking Pluto they don't dare to express it. They need a lot of encouragement to express their ideas.

The split Pluto of the fifth house is: you are unhappy because you want to be happy that much. You throw your own happiness away. Enjoying holidays might be a problem. The exotic tropic atmosphere of an unknown culture is overseen and you are only irritated by the lack of organization, the heat, the mud and the dirt, the insects, the air conditioner that does not work and all other inconveniences during the trip. It all comes down to a suppressed lust for life. Also on the sexual plane this blocking might occur. Making love suddenly all appetite fades away for no reason. Having a date you think over and over again whether you want it or not. If the caution wins you throw a beautiful opportunity away. If you go for it chances are big you block during the pairing dance. Or they get off too fast. If the spontaneity breaks through a mighty Plutonic energy is released 'too big to handle'. An uncontrollable energy takes over. It takes you over completely and that is the fear. The way to overcome it is: 'relax, be happy and don't worry'. But for a native with Pluto in the fifth house this is the hardest thing. Another feature of Pluto in the fifth house is the porn issue. Or they are deadly against pornography and the sex business. Or they are holy preachers of sexual freedom and have a job in the porn industry. Which side are you on? For Pluto in the fifth house there is no middle way.

For most natives with Pluto in the fifth house having children is a hard affair. The split is: you want to be a perfect parent and at the same time you feel unable to get real contact. The moment your child is nagging you panic. You blame yourself for not being able to understand your child, to share his world. Having thought deeply about it you try to talk it out in a serious manner. In fact you want to learn something from your child. Otherwise why would you question him about his behavior? The child does not understand it either. He does not understand your worries. The positions are swapped. Your child has to explain things to you instead of the other way around. Instinctively your child starts to manipulate you. I have heard saying that children break your ego. For a parent with Pluto in the fifth house this is true. Somehow there is always a problem to be stressed about. That is how your child has power over you. They feel and manipulate your anxiousness. You are the slave of your child. You love your child too much. You are not able to be yourself with him. You think you are a bad parent. In most cases this is absolutely not true. On the contrary by your worries you are an excellent parent.

It might happen to your own shock that you start to despise your child. How unthankful they are. You realize how badly disappointed you are by your child. Again and again you torture yourself with the thought of being a bad parent. It is your fault he became like that. Sometimes your child is indeed a rat. It is your karmic fate to be his parent. But more often you have too high of expectations for your child.

Natives with Pluto in the fifth house always experience some kind of problem with their children one way or the other. Sometimes silly problems but also big problems. A woman consulted me because her ex-husband managed to take her son away by law. She was not allowed to meet him anymore. Another woman having Pluto in the fifth house wrote me an angry e-mail pointing out to me she had not a single problem with children: "She has had three abortions and she did not care at all!" No problem? So why does she write me that e-mail? This is an example of how Pluto problems are unmentionable.

Cracking Pluto in the fifth house means a return to your passion. Transit Pluto is passing the eighth house which means passion. You rejuvenate yourself. You'll enjoy a second youth. You fall in love again. It might be a person awakening you sexually. Someone kissed the sleeping beauty and she came to life. And then she became wild too. A dazzling occurrence that changed everything. Everybody in town knows. That's the thing: to be open about it.

Basically it is a change in socializing. To love doing things together for the joy of it. To enjoy doing things for no reason. Just for the fun: music, sports, nature, metaphysical things, travelling or theatre. You join a club: a chorus, a drama club, the local brass band, cookery art, or whatever group that is about creating things to show the public. There you'll meet yourself. There you can be the clown proposing your wildest ideas. Having to do the performance you get stage fright. You die a thousand deaths. All those people watching, your family, your neighbors even some business associates. What if I goof off? Eternal shame will be your part. Since walking away is no option you crack Pluto and realize how easy it is and even more how much fun it is. In the next times the stage fright will die out.

Suppose you are rich you can start a theater or arthouse and invite artists. You create together with those artists. It is no sin to have a sexual escapade with one of your volunteers. Follow your creativity. You become popular and that is the quantum leap, your release. It is no sin to be popular. Nobody will guillotine you out of jealousy. You step into the art business and your product has to be presented to the public. Cracking Pluto in the fifth house means you crack your fear for public disapproval.

By virtue of preferring a place in the shade natives with Pluto in the fifth house might rise to the top. At the top they are in the middle of the attention. They are asked to do roadshows and to handle the media. That is another way to crack Pluto. If they say something everybody is holding their breath. All eyes are directed to you about what your plans are and what you say. Your popularity is at stake. It is causing sleepless nights. What am I going to say? Being afraid of a scandal they prepare themselves well. They are hard to tackle. But is that fun? That is holding in. Cracking Pluto is to break through and dare to be the flamboyant entrepreneur winding everybody around his finger with his jokes, sharp reactions and his original plans. It is not something you can learn. It is your hidden power. It is possible this goes automatically, forced by the situation. When your plan is shot off you create a new plan on the spot with a big smile and don't get personally hurt by it.

For all natives with Pluto in the fifth house cracking Pluto has to do with their children. If they are taken away from you, you make sure you get them back. If you have had three abortions you give birth to one. Those are the heavy cases. More often you get problems when your children leave home. After all those years you created a bond with your child. Now he is gone you are worrying if he is doing well. It is hard to let go. But you have got to set them free. When they are gone your mansion gets awfully quiet. You want them to visit you more frequently and want to have a say about their decisions. You need to realize they have become adults and they have got their own agenda. More than ever you have to treat them as equals. If you don't and you put them under pressure to come home and you paternalise them on their lifestyle you will lose. They are not your possession. It is the trick to not tense up in emotions when they visit you. You need someone or something else to focus on to fill up your lonely hours. This means you begin a new hobby or join a brass band or something like that. It means time is freed to fulfil your wildest ideas.

Cracking Pluto in the fifth house works out twofold. The nerds will learn to be wild and the party trippers will find their silent space. In almost all cases it means modesty and unpretentious amusement. If you have a job in the entertainment business where love is a trademark you seriously fall in love. Finally you found somebody who makes you feel completely at ease. You buy a yacht and you organize boat trips with a few personal friends, far away from all that noise. It is the little things that make the fun.
Or suppose you are a professor you organize on Sundays a philosophers club with a group of trustees where you can talk freely without any taboos. The ideas are born there. This outlet results in a general relaxation.

Cracking Pluto in the fifth house also might happen gradually. Gradually you loosen up. Slowly you express yourself easier. More and more you become playful and you allow yourself to tell a joke or ask attention for a story. Suppose you are a big shot and everybody looks up to you. You begin to realize you can't do anything wrong anymore. There is no need to worry anymore. Your mood gets better and you become more enjoyable. You go to your work singing. Instantaneously you tell your ideas in the meetings. No beforehand thoughts or tactics, the ideas are born in the moment itself. They won't nail you down on your ideas.

They won't dare. Without all those restrictions also a lot of humor and fun will be released.

Pluto in the sixth house

Pluto in the sixth house is all about duty. The world is a grand mess with an endless array of problems. Who is responsible? Pluto in the sixth house means a fear and a drive the moment you stand for a task, the moment you have to accomplish a goal. You cramp up when you have got to do something. Basically it comes down to a fear of failure.

Born with Pluto in the sixth house you have past life memories facing a mission impossible with catastrophic results. You were in a hopeless situation, a catch 22 situation. For example you were born a slave with no way out. You had to work yourself to death. Now in this life you still think you have to work yourself to death or you revolt against it. Or as a youngster you had to care for and defend your family. You gave your life in vain. As a doctor you tried to save the population from the pestilence. Instead you died yourself on pestilence in the middle of the dying. Now in this life you get a hopeless feeling the moment you feel responsible for something or someone.

In general in a past life you were overpowered. You thought you had to save the world. You tried hard against all odds and you succumbed. Helplessly you watched the disaster taking place. No way was it your fault but …… you have got the feeling that you screwed it up. You should have tried harder.

With Pluto in the sixth house you have a drive to stand for the things you have to do and a fear of failure. The moment you stand for a task you get a stress and all the conditions for the next failure are created. The split is: you have a great working power and organisational talent but you hate it too.

When the drive is bigger than the fear you become a slave, working your balls off for the company, for your money, for your duty. You lose yourself in the goals you set. You think it is all your responsibility and it all depends on you. It becomes over important. You can't let go. You work too hard. This stress eventually will lead to a burn out. Natives with Pluto in the sixth house get a burn out at least one time in their life. You were not able to distinguish your own responsibilities (for your health) and the shared responsibilities of your job.

Is the fear bigger you avoid any responsibility. You run away when something should be done. You pass the buck, driven by a resistance to accept your responsibilities to do what you should do. Let the other do the dirty work. If something should be done you don't even start on it. You think beforehand that you are not able. You need a lot of encouragement to get something done, if not a big stick, to get your ass going.

In rare cases someone with Pluto in the sixth house suffers health problems and needs a strict discipline to cope with it, like diets or tough medical schemes. This is special karma. Most likely you had a similar disease in a past life.

Children with Pluto in the sixth house are very obedient. They try to match the expectations of the parents and join the household. Pretty soon they get stressed on this matter. If the fear is bigger they give up helping and they hide. If they have to clean up their mess they walk away. When they have to do the dishes they find all the arguments not to do it. They develop all kinds of tricks to pass the family duties on to their brothers and sisters. They fall into mighty struggles about who has to do what. If they can't win the argument they simply walk away. They want no responsibilities anymore. They develop strategies to find an easy way out for every task they are confronted with. Later this attitude might wind up as sheer junky behaviour. They become parasites on others.

More frequently however they become the domestic drudge. They feel responsible for all family affairs. When something has to be done and nobody wants to do it, they will do it. They are apt to be abused. If not by the parents, then by their sisters and brothers, nieces and nephews. They will also have problems with neighbourhood children and at school. All of them all notice how easy it is to put them on a job. They sense it and mercilessly exploit it. As a parent you should be aware of this and protect your child. At least you should point out to him or her how this manipulation works. In vain of course, because Pluto forces are irrational but it could prevent worse things.

With Pluto in the sixth house you constantly get sucked into discussions about who is supposed to do what, a fight about division of labour. The polar result is either you do all the work and the other sits in his lazy chair, doing nothing, or it is the other way around.

At school children with Pluto in the sixth house do their stinking best. They have a drive to do everything as well as possible. You might think: 'Excellent, so they get only A's.' But that's not the case. Mostly they get C's or a C minus and they pass the course by the skin or their teeth. The fear of failing is choking and confuses their mind. They are middle men. A lot of them don't go for a top education. They go for less for a fear of failure.

With Pluto in the sixth house you find your Plutonic fears in your occupation. You always worry, preparing yourself for the worst. They are gold for the company because of their reliability. They give more than is asked for. Somehow they feel an ultimate responsibility on their shoulders like they are the boss themselves although they are just an employee. In job delineations they accept tasks that are too heavy. If a colleague fails to do his job they will do it. If their boss is mixed up they will repair the damage. Their job is totally absorbing them. And that's the trap. They don't complain, they don't ask for help, they just make sure the job is done. Some people with Pluto in the sixth house think working for the money is the holiest thing on earth. At home they cannot relax because of the problems at work. They can't let go. They are overcommitted. If you have an employee with Pluto in the sixth house you can leave the shop in his hands and go on holiday to the Bahama's. He will put his back into it. You are laying at the beach drinking the fanciest cocktails and he works hard for your company bringing in the money. But don't forget to come home regularly because when he gets overworked and falls into a burn out without you knowing it, you might lose everything.

Natives with Pluto in the sixth house should never be given the final responsibility for a project before they have cracked Pluto. But a lot of times it happens. Still they often start their own company or you are made head of a department. Their fear of failure chases them. Their life scheme changes in a 80 hours a week job. The job takes them over completely. They don't go home until the work is done. Somehow they need to double check everything. They can't delegate. Deep down there is a distrust in the integrity of their partners. If a job is done poorly, they personally redo it. They want to be 200% sure that everything is in order. So they run and organise without a pause. In the beginning it will all go fine, even excellent, but in the long run they can't keep it up. Finally they collapse. It is all too energy consuming. They get a burn out. What is feared will happen. They get bankrupt, they are put off the job or they fall ill. Even worse, nobody likes them anymore because they are working robots. The split is: you carry the responsibility for everything and everybody accept for yourself, passing the limits of your abilities.

A Pluto in the sixth house employee needs a manager to tell him what to do and even more what not to do. A Pluto in the sixth house person fits best when he plays the second fiddle. He needs someone to define his task. He needs a tap on his back as a reassurance that he is doing well. He needs a manager who protects him against himself. Give him a few days off to recover ...... after the work is done of course. Some natives with Pluto in the sixth house go to bed with their superior or colleague for a better cooperation at work. That is how important their job is. In some cases it can lead to a good marriage after all.

Another extreme is the parasite type with Pluto in the sixth house who needs a bit too much guidance. You have to explain to them ten times how to do something. Despite all the supervision they goof off constantly. Sure they do their best. Their fear to be a misfit comes true. Somehow they seem to not understand what it is all about. It comes down to a misunderstanding about the structures of life. Not being able to discern side-lines and headlines. So your boss will finally sack you, not for no reason. Some women are looking for a rich and brilliant man as a husband. So they don't have to do anything anymore for the rest of their life. The more simple ones might choose for a carpenter. That is handy for all the plumbing and odd jobs around the house. If something needs to be done their man will do it. If such relation ends a lot of problems might arise because they became the owner of all their man has achieved. He wants his share and threatens to commit a crime if you don't pay him.

With Pluto in the sixth house a confusion occurs between formal and informal, between work and private things. Your job becomes so important you completely identify yourself with it. You only talk about your shop and nothing else counts anymore. At home they can't relax and forget about their job. Some natives with Pluto in the sixth house run their family life like they are running a firm. Strict schemes are designed how of how to deal with each other. Sunday morning at breakfast the family tasks for the next week are on the agenda. In the long run nobody likes that. Eventually your spouse and children will revolt and turn their backs on you. Some women with Pluto in the sixth house consider being a housewife as their job. In family affairs they take all the responsibilities. They make sure their man, children and all their relatives are served well. They have the feeling that they have shortcomings (fear of failure) in their marriage. They carry the can for everyone and everybody and they don't get the credit for it. Or: their husband is rich, their bed is well made but they still want to do something. They want to be useful. They have no structure. It drives them crazy. During the cracking Pluto period of soul-searching and wondering they finally come to the conclusion that, when it comes to down to it: *in the end everyone bears his own responsibilities*. That is the relieve.

In general natives with Pluto in the sixth house are of good health. Pluto is a main indicator of disease. That counts for everyone. Still there is a point here. If a native with Pluto in the sixth house catches a cold they cramp up on how to heal it. A lot of times they suppress their illness and deny it because of a resistance, a fear, to take the body seriously. If you are sick you can't do your work anymore. They don't want to know it. If they work too hard and the body gives all kinds of signals that it is exhausted they just push on. They don't listen to their body, they control it. 'Suddenly' they get sick. They are ashamed of their illness and don't want anybody to know. It takes a long time before they go to the doctor. Some are afraid of the doctor. A doctor gives you horrible news and bitter pills. A doctor is an authority. Going to a doctor they do exactly, without thinking, what he says. They expect to get some pills and everything will be all right. But when the pills don't work the doctor is to blame and becomes the bogeyman. Now you have to become your own doctor, which is cracking Pluto.

Basically the problem is how to be your own doctor. An example of being overanxious about health problems is the man who got the flu. For a week he was bound at home suffering with a high fever. Needless to say not being able to show up at your job is the worst thing there is. After he recovered he immediately decided for 'safety reasons' to get a flu shot because he never wanted to experience such a thing again, not realising he had already built up flu resistance during his fever.

Cracking Pluto in the sixth house means a transformation in dealing with responsibilities. In most cases transiting Pluto will be passing through the ninth house which is about philosophy, about understanding life. What are you living for? Your burn out makes you think. You realize there are limits to your helpfulness, loyalty and working power. You get the insight everyone eventually is responsible for himself. They were leaning too much on you. You were living too much to fulfil in the expectations of others. It had become a habit to call on you. So with or without a burn out an irritation builds up when they call on you again. You were not able to say 'no'. Cracking Pluto means you learn to say: "No, help yourself! Bye." Each one is responsible for his own thing. Next time you'll be strong and you won't jump in when someone is failing. This not only counts for your job but also for your family life. Have you been the housewife always taking the work out of the hands of your husband and children? Now you stop doing that. Or the other way around, your family makes it perfectly clear that your over-concern is not accepted anymore. They consider you nosey. Mind your own business. They don't tell you anymore what they are doing. You'll be forced to understand it. It might be you realize you always took care of your family although they were lacking nothing. During cracking Pluto you change your attitude. When your children again want you to do something for them you say firmly: "A fifteen year old teenager should be able to do things without help. Do it yourself." And you stick to it no matter how much they are nagging. This can lead to major tensions because you have to break through a behaviour pattern. A pattern where everybody expects you to be the drudge. You don't want it anymore and besides you don't have the energy anymore. The agony is that you get blamed for your refusal. "Are you still with us?" The cracking of Pluto is you going through those fears and letting it happen.

In this period your concept of life is transforming. There is a change deep in your soul. You doubt very much whether it is good what you do. The fear of failure again knocks at your door. 'Did I do everything wrong?' You might be afraid they will turn against you. You have to go through it. It takes some time to get your philosophy clear but when you finally have sorted it out you are there. As a result you set your own priorities. It will take a while until they get used to it. Eventually it will be a great relief.

At work cracking Pluto in the sixth house is all about having trust in your staff and knowing how to delegate. Suppose you have a high position. You grew to be vital for the company and without your consent nothing is possible. You are indispensable. Chances are high you are a control freak constantly checking to see that the job is well done. In the end this distrust will not be appreciated. In the period of cracking Pluto your box of tricks is not accepted anymore. Behind your back they are conspiring against you. You are considered an impersonal working robot. The only things you do are organizing, selling and buying. Who are you yourself? As a result literally everybody suddenly turns against you and you get the worst thing that can happen: you get the sack. You are promoted off. You are set on the side-line.

Common thing is: you get a burnout. It all became too big, too much. You collapse. You can't go anymore. Your body refuses. You get sick and have to stay home. The fiction of being pivotal blows up and you get left on the side-line. By cosmic intervention you are forced to transform your sense of duty. Your burnout is not the end of the world. To your surprise the enterprise was not hurt by your burnout. Knowing this (ninth house) your work and your life get much more enjoyable and easier. You will be also more effective because the pressure is gone. Without any stress you learn how to delegate. To your own big relief you find out who you can trust. You find out by trying. It is all about trust. That way your joy of life comes back and you will be ready for the big stuff. Remember Pluto is a power. Checking out every detail is too time consuming.

Suppose those calamities did not occur and you always have been obediently working as a middleman. You always left the responsibility to your manager. You will find out during cracking Pluto you will be asked to take the lead. You will be offered a big promotion. Or you will be challenged to start your own firm. You have proven your integrity for such a long time. They trust you. In that case you have got to say 'yes'. For natives with Pluto in the sixth house the time to be the top director is after cracking of Pluto. Overcome your fear of failure and say 'yes'. Just do it. You figure out the plans and your team executes it. The Pluto transformation is to trust yourself and even more: to trust your team. A Pluto in the sixth house native always is a doer. You need an issue to concentrate on and something to care for. Cracking Pluto is a transformation in the way you do it.

Cracking Pluto in the sixth house means an opening up of your body consciousness. Suppose you always denied your body signals. Now you cannot deny them anymore. The control locked up in your body explodes, in the beginning without any control. Your burnout (or even worse) is helping you to connect with your body again. All those body tensions need to be released. Asking the doctor for some other pills is useless. During the cracking of Pluto you learn to listen to your body. Take your time for your body. Love your body. When you are tired stop running around. Enough is enough. You'll find out it all becomes easier.

If you have been struggling all your life with a mysterious disease you will be put on the spot to give your body all the attention it needs. You might be balancing on the edge of dying. You'll be forced to really connect with your body, speak with your body, ask your body and listen to your body. You have to do it all yourself. No one else can do that for you. You have got to find the clues yourself. Of course you can use all the medical advice possible but you must still do it yourself. If you survive it, it will be a win forever. It will not come back, not even in future lives. If you succumb you'll get a chance in a future life to try it again. Finally it is all about being your own authority, your own doctor. A cracked Pluto in the sixth house is the unofficial doctor of the cosmos.

Pluto in the seventh house

Natives with Pluto in the seventh house get anxious the moment they get a relationship. You have got a drive for a perfect relationship and at the same time a fear that it will not work out. Your longing for a perfect relationship is 'too big to handle'. Having a relationship is a must no matter how. Living alone is unthinkable. Without a relationship you are panicking. In relating natives with Pluto in the seventh house meet a misbalance of power. They are basically on the defense. Much is due to feelings of dependence. You can consider a relationship as a square with a straight line in the middle. One side is your territory and the other side is the territory of your partner. When two people meet this line starts moving and meandering by the coiling of the aura's. The territory of natives with Pluto in the seventh house will shrink and the territory of the partner will expand until he has got it all. This loss of territory unfolds in two possible ways.

1) Either you keep on pushing your partner until he doesn't listen anymore. The relationship is a heavy fighting one with one hell of a row after another.

2) You are always quiet and accept everything your partner does.

The Plutonic stress in relating stems from past lives. Within a marriage something went totally wrong. Being married was a love-hate relationship ending up in a violent hell. Although your husband beat you a lot, you knew he did love you. After he clubbed you to death he regretted and cried bitter tears. Or: you were given in marriage for family policies and you were very lonely your entire life. Or: although you loved your husband you constantly committed adultery. Finally he committed suicide and everybody in town despised you. Those kind of past life experiences created a will to do better in this life. In this life you want a perfect marriage. Another reason for being born with Pluto in the seventh house is an unfinished love affair. You two were madly in love and suddenly you were cruelly separated. Your lover was killed in front of your eyes. You never got over this catastrophe and you are longing for this ultimate lover again. Or: you were courted by a nice man of good family but you refused. The man committed suicide and you regretted for the rest of your life having refused him. Or you were happily married but when your partner died you became awfully lonely. In this life you are afraid for being alone again and a relationship must come to your rescue.

In all cases natives with Pluto in the seventh house long for a perfect marriage. This stress makes it so hard to get. Your relationship is your most precious thing. You can't really be yourself in a relationship. There is no relaxation. You are constantly focused on the other. You're anticipating what he thinks, likes and needs. You try to fulfill his dreams as a perfect match. From a distance you manipulate to please your partner, to make him happy, to support him in his job ….. to control him. As long as your partner is happy you are doing a good job. But you yourself, you don't feel free. You are not really able to tell what you want. When there is an argument you get lost in the negotiations. Maybe in the beginning you stand firm, if not overreacting, but if the disagreement lasts you cave in. You are afraid it would be the end of the relationship. You don't want to put your marriage at stake. Unconsciously you feel emotionally blackmailed for no reason. You give in on your own territory and you give your power out of your hands. This is a creeping process. When you are mad you don't allow yourself to be mad. You should be perfect. Isn't it? So by the time your partner finds out he can do whatever he wants he has snatched your territory. Natives with Pluto in the seventh house meet their authority problem in their partner. They look for a strong partner. Next they get dominated by this strong partner.

Natives with Pluto in the seventh house simply have got to have a relation. It begins in high school. Without a relation there is no status. They make sure they can show off with their boyfriend. Often they marry early. Falling in love is overwhelming and they have got to have that person. Once they have it they immediately want children and think it is forever. But beware. A lot of natives with Pluto in the seventh house don't marry out of love but out of calculation, or both. At a young age they carefully watch and judge who is the best. They want only the best. They spot their prey and use all kinds of manipulations to get him (or her). If they don't succeed they spot another until they do succeed. And then rose garden should begin ......
A lot of natives with Pluto in the seventh house wind up with a dominating and demanding partner. They wanted the best and they got the best: a hell of a man or a beauty queen with a higher mind, just as they picture their hero to be. After the puppy love, the disenchantment sets in. But with Pluto in the seventh house you are not able to face it. Although your partner is a despot without any consideration, you continue the relationship. And that is how it started. You wanted him/her so bad, you allowed him everything from the beginning. So after a few years you are completely under their thumb. You accept everything as

long as the relationship continues. Your position becomes worse and worse. Then he tells you he has a new love, a young beauty he really can have fun with. He is happier than ever. You realize there is nothing you can do. The question is: divorce or not. Cracking Pluto is standing up for yourself, do not accept it anymore. Stand up for your position even if it means divorce. But that is awfully difficult for natives with Pluto in the seventh house.

The stress in relating basically unfolds in one of two ways:

1) A minority get a relationship with a lot of fighting. You try to control your partner. He has got to behave the way you want. If not you press him in any way. All kinds of power tactics are used out of fear of things getting out of hand. To the outside world you pretend to have a perfect marriage but the moment you two are alone the struggle begins. For example: You two are at a party having fun and showing off how well you two go together. Everybody thinks: 'What a nice couple. See, how happy they are.' And indeed, during the party you two are one great harmony. The moment you come home the struggle begins: "And you said this and that. You can't do that. What the hell do you think? Next time .... !" Next morning the whole argument seems to be forgotten. In extreme cases the relationship turns into a 'Who is afraid for the Virginia Woolf' syndrome. You break each other off to the bone but somehow breaking up is not an option. At the end your partner is not taking you seriously anymore and the same thing will happen as in case two: Behind your back he goes his own way.

2) Most natives with Pluto in the seventh house feel at ease when their partner takes the lead. Their partner does the

talking and makes the decisions. After a while their partner finds out he never gets counter pressure and he can do whatever he wants. As long as your partner is a reasonable and fine person with a shining personality nothing is wrong. But this is utopia. Out of predestination your partner will eventually do the forbidden thing: abuse his/her position. So you have to get along with awkward situations in your marriage. Things which make you unhappy. Years later the pain and sorrow will burst out. Before you pushed it away. In the worst case your partner loses all his respect and keeps on misbehaving himself (adultery) and you don't dare to say or do anything about it.

Only in rare cases he or she will not abuse the situation. I have heard stories of natives with Pluto in the seventh house who were married to a fantastic person who always did the right thing. Her entire life she did not have anything to complain about. The problem began when he died. No one compares to him. And she entered the dark tunnel of not having a relationship and idealizing her ex-partner.

Men with Pluto in the seventh house often marry demanding women. They spot a woman resembling their mother. They want a beauty queen, the top of the bill. From the beginning he is like wax in her hands. After a few years of marriage he can't fulfill her dreams anymore. For example: Being a dull clerk with a high financial education you married a wild beauty, a model too. After a few years your marriage has changed into a daily routine of having your job and raising the children. Your marriage has petered out and you don't realize it. Although she explained it to you so many times you seemed to be deaf. You don't know how to blow new energy in your marriage. And then it happens: She tells you she has another lover and wants a divorce. Oh, shock. It feels like being killed. By all means you try to avoid divorce. You accept her having another relation. That is how good you are. For years you are tortured waiting for her when she spends her time with her lover. Finally the divorce comes as a release leaving the question: How come you did not divorce her years ago.

Women with Pluto in the seventh house often marry a relentless man. A man who knows what is best for her and keeping her short. An intimidating man who thinks he is always right. A man who does not allow her anything. A man to be handled with velvet gloves. A man who draws his own plan. A man who treats everybody like his subordinate. They kept on playing the ideal woman for him. When the question of divorce is raised they panic. Later, on the therapist couch, they sigh: 'If I had only the guts to leave him ten years before. I would have spared myself a lot of misery. I threw ten years of my life away'. And they have a hard time erasing the memories of that terrible man.

One of the tragic lots which hit natives with Pluto in the seventh house is when their spouse tells them they have another lover. He/she demands a divorce because it is over. What would you do? With Pluto in the seventh house you pretend to accepts it but underneath they don't. They can't. Your spouse is the dominant factor so you must accept it. Like an ideal partner you are helpful to arrange the divorce, about the kids, the financial stuff, etc. At the end of the negotiations when the divorce is awfully near you collapse. You get a nervous breakdown. You get sick. No doctor has a medication. You weep and you wail. You beg your spouse to come home and to draw back the decision. You go on your knees. You crawl in the dust to save your marriage. Your spouse did not foresee this and gets in a fright. He/she does not want to be responsible for your suicide. So, the divorce is blown off. But now you really have no position anymore. Your spouse will only despise you more. Your spouse keeps his/her lover and you are the fifth wheel on the wagon. This can last for years. And nobody knows. You and your spouse are keeping it secret: such a shame. To the outside world you keep up appearances being such a nice couple but in the meanwhile your marriage is a hell. The cracking of Pluto is to fully realize the situation and divorce. In the end the divorce is only postponed. This hell had to last that long because it needed this time. You simply needed this time to wake up.

You might think: 'Is this not a bit too extreme? Is this really true?' In a lot of cases it is that extreme. It is hidden. It is kept secret. It is shameful. Only after the calamity, during the cracking of Pluto, is it to be talked about.

Most natives with Pluto in the seventh house go through a painful marriage. Afterwards they wonder why it had to last that long. Why they did not break off the relationship at the beginning of the troubles? It might take a while before they start a new relationship but they will. The aim of Pluto in the seventh house is to overcome your karmic relationship problems so the next relationship must follow. And this will be a bond in which they can be their selves and have their own space.

Also at work Pluto in the seventh house natives meet their power in relating with their colleagues. Too long they wait with their complaints. Too long they push away their irritation. Only because they don't want problems. So they get stuck with work nobody wants to do because they want to keep up the good relations. If a workmate is harassing them they don't know how to respond. They keep silent. The irrational part is: If there is no collegiality why are you so fraternal yourself. You don't defend your territory. So it might happen that a tremendous tension builds up in the labor relations. They get overstrained because they don't speak out. You are insecure whether your irritation is justified and your criticism will turn against you. The answer to get out of your isolation is: overthrow your fears and speak out. Talking is the only way.

Cracking Pluto in the seventh house means you become more direct in your interaction with your partner. Transiting Pluto goes through the tenth house so you get challenged to take the lead. Your reputation and position (tenth house) is at stake. You should be taken seriously by your spouse as a lesson to be your own authority. When transiting Pluto was visiting your ninth house you thought you had to behave like a model puppet. When Pluto goes through the tenth house you set your own rules of relating. Cracking Pluto in the seventh house is a transformation in relating. From now on your relationship will be the way you want it and nothing else. If again a fundamental disagreement arises on how to deal with each other you stick to your point. Either your marriage transforms the way you want it to or it is over. You stand firm in your decision, as you told them so, because he/she has to take you seriously. And don't swap sides at the last minute. Saving your marriage is only possible when your spouse is open to it. He should be able to discuss his behavior and transform too. But mostly your spouse is used to your submissive attitude and does not realize your transformation. He simply stays in his pattern. So most commonly divorce is the result. The fear you have to overcome is that you have to get along without your ex although you think you are not able to. Cracking Pluto in the seventh house is finding out living as a single is not that bad. If you meet somebody out of that position it will be much easier to relate.

After the crash a lot of natives with Pluto in the seventh house decide not to live together anymore. They finally got rid of their ex and never again. They have got enough by their selves. Still a relationship is tempting. You still want a relationship but it's not that compulsory. Being alone after the divorce is tough but you have got to cope with it. If you meet someone special after all those years you will be much more cautious. You are clear about your do's and dont's and what you want. It could be another marriage but not necessarily. You say: "I would like to share my life with you but I have my own agenda." So you two simply adjust to each other's agenda. If that is not possible it is no problem because there is no compelling dream to fulfill. After cracking of Pluto in the seventh house relating becomes easy and fun.

During cracking Pluto in the seventh house the imbalance of power in your relationship will come to a climax. You do the unthinkable. You call up the lover of your spouse and tell this ape loud and clearly: "If you once again meet with my spouse you'll be a dead duck." To your spouse you say: "You don't want to quit your adultery? Well, go then." If that does not help and he/she sticks to his habits, you stick to your words and throw him/her out. It is hard and it feels like dying but it is a new beginning. You succumb to your fears to be alone because you know living alone is better than this hell. For your self-esteem it is important to organize it yourself (transiting Pluto in the tenth house). When the other organizes the divorce you crack Pluto the hard way, namely not on your conditions. Important thing is to find allies. You need people to share. Keeping up appearances means you are lost. When you don't know what to do anymore, ask for help and advice. Talk about it with friends or professional advisers. In time of trouble you find out your real friends. When you don't ask nobody knows. When you talk around you'll get help from unexpected sides.

When you have learned to be direct in your interaction with everybody you relate to and you are able to hold on to your directness (cracking Pluto is a continuous thing) your weakness transforms into power. The moment an imbalance in power occurs you notice and you don't let it happen. Diplomatic and without affronting you lay your finger on the problem, easily and frankly. This makes you untouchable. Before cracking Pluto you used to get upset in those situations nervously seeking an easy way out. Now you stand firm in your opinion in all reasonableness. Also at work you will grow in your power while cracking Pluto. Once a colleague is harassing you again you stand up for yourself. Remember to get allies. Play it high if necessary. Go to the personnel or legal department. Your power is reasonableness. Explain it and they'll be at your side. After your victory you'll be treated as a VIP. Sometimes you might think: 'It is not that bad.' For example when a colleague likes you too much and constantly draws your attention. Cracking Pluto means you make it clear once and for all to stop with that childish behavior. You will gain a reputation. By gaining a reputation you become gold for your company because you'll be able to negotiate in labor conflicts. That is part of the power of Pluto in the seventh house. You know all about those ego power games. You know what moves them. Now that you are taken seriously you have the power to tell them: "That is not the way, this is the way." Before you used to sit on the fence but now you dare to take sides because you care.

Some natives with Pluto in the seventh house have to crack Pluto when their partner deceases. Since their twenties they lived with their dream partner who was always right. For forty years he was their help and stay. Now that he deceased at his 60th (a bit too soon) it gets tough. Loneliness is knocking on the door. So they have to crack Pluto at this advanced age. You long for the warmth and togetherness you used to share but nobody is good enough. Now you have to stand for your own decisions. Often they still feel the presence of their deceased partner. That is beautiful. That helps. The problem is not to get depressive. Don't retreat in loneliness. Relate with your friends. Feel what they mean for you. It is the power of Pluto in the seventh house to understand the relationship you have with each individual you meet.

Pluto in the eighth house

With Pluto in the eighth house you have a drive and a fear for intimacy. There is a tremendous commitment, 'too big to handle'. So you hold in. When you fall in love you fall obsessively in love. You are unsure about what moves the other, why he does what he does, spinning the weirdest theories about her behavior. Since you don't dare to talk about it you investigate sideways to find out. You are afraid for wrong intentions. You don't trust your own observations. Once you set your mind about somebody you stick to it. You idolize your beloved one and you are blind to her wrong doings. You get emotionally upset, shocked or even raging mad, when your eyes are opened and your beloved one is different from what you thought. On the other hand when you commit yourself to somebody your commitment is total and warm. You can mean a lot for someone. Natives with Pluto in the eighth house hold in their power for transformation. You stick to patterns too long. You can't handle sudden changes like death or birth. It takes too long to find out people have changed. The other way around: they might have an urge to change people. But the tension is too big to handle. You don't directly say: "Hey, don't you think this is bad behavior for yourself?" No, you wind curves to make him change. If someone has changed you find out to late, blind for the fact he has already changed. All out of an excess of love.

Being born with Pluto in the eighth house means you have had a fatal love affair in a past life. Lots of times it deals with 'crîme passionel'. You killed or have been killed by the one you loved so much. How pure was your love? Often it had to do with jealousy. As a women you poisoned the mistresses of your man. As a man you killed your lover on the spot when she told you she was going to marry some-one else. You were condemned by the locals having a love affair with a bad man. You knew he was not bad but finally they jumped on him and on you too. Or: You witnessed how your girlfriend was offered to the gods by your own people because of her beauty.

So if you tell a native with Pluto in the eighth house that you love her she might get mad. Where have I heard that before? That was in a past life when you were killed by your lover. In general Pluto in the eighth house refers to an emotional shock in a past life concerning love and loyalty, sex and intimacy, which still lingers on in your memory. The result is a drive and a fear for a passionate love, hoping things go well this time.

Children with Pluto in the eighth house are very emotion-al. Inevitably a process is set in motion where they hold in on their emotions. The child feels easily betrayed. A fear grows to express what you feel and want. A distance and distrust is created out of fear your love and emotions will be abused. They get scared for intimacy. Crucial is in high school when they fall in love for the first time. They are overwhelmed by their emotions but still have to do the right thing.

With Pluto in the eighth house you desperately want to share someone's deepest secrets. Doing so your own emo-tions get too intense and you don't know how to approach the other. If you approach someone you do it with an iron grip on your emotions. The moment you love somebody you hold in. When you are approached you seem to be ice cold. But that is a lonely affair while you long so much for affection.

A man develops all kind of manipulating techniques. You try to find out how she wants you to behave. You manipulate and turn around to be in tune. You don't put your cards on the table and you hold back until you are real sure. Once they got an eye on someone they make sure they get it too with iron discipline and patience. Women with Pluto in the eighth house have flaws of being obsessively in love. Their way of approach is dominant. Their manipulation is to go along with whatever the other does especially on the sexual plane. Nothing goes too far. You idolize your lover and agree on everything he does.

The emotions natives with Pluto in the eighth house go through when they feel committed concerns not only a lover but could also be family, children, pupils, colleagues or …. anyone you feel committed to. The way they handle it is roughly threefold.

1) They get frightened and hold off. A strange anger or distrust sets in when a love affair is hanging in the air. They don't relate or only by mistake.

2) They fall in love, start a relationship but the relationship somehow dries out for lack of intimacy.

3) They throw themselves obsessively into a love affair blind about the real nature of their lover.

1) If the fear for commitment is the winner, natives with Pluto in the eighth house don't really dare to come to an in-depth understanding. That's too 'big to handle'. They become formal and superficial. They lose their insight of the human nature. They only notice the outside. If they are married they have made a set of arrangements about their marriage and they don't think about it anymore. 'That's

settled' they think and they focus for their work. They are unreachable. They manipulate the potentials of others (eighth house). Quite often they are moneygrubbers. Their financial situation is their final security, being greedy in the name of god, masters in exploiting people, masters in squeezing people out.

2) A problem of natives with Pluto in the eighth house is to follow the evolution of their love affair. Nothing stays the same also not the nature of your love. The evolution of your soul is not necessarily the same as your partner's. Only very late, too late, you realize your lover has changed. For years you were in a deadlock and you didn't realize. Your partner tried and tried to make you understand but you closed up. One day she is gone. Or the other way around: After the puppy love you realize you don't really love your partner that much. Suddenly by some event the feeling is gone. How confusing. He/she is still in the seventh heaven with you. You don't dare to say it. You did give your word didn't you? The relationship dries out. This can last for years, for decennia. There is no intimacy anymore, not to mention sexual intercourse. Nothing happens and your love has been turned into a dead flower. You stopped sharing your wild instincts with your best friend. The problem is you don't dare to face it and you let it be. Parting is a hard and a very emotional thing.

A problem some women might suffer as a result of Pluto in the eighth house is frigidity. After years of making love with a person you actually don't love your body revolts. You get a sickness on your sexual organs. Or: you want obsessively to be a perfect lover. You make love by the thought and not by your instincts with the same result: Your hormone household gets screwed up. Part of the problem is woman with Pluto in the eighth house tend to be sexually overruled by their partner because they are afraid to say 'no'. You don't dare to say: "Hey, this is going too far." Unconsciously you are afraid he'll get mad. When he gets mad you are afraid the same thing will happen that happened in a past life: Sheer violence and goodbye forever. Men have the same problems but it's harder to sexually abuse them when it does not get up.

3) Another feature of Pluto in the eighth house is falling obsessively in love without any control. You get that relationship but after a few months or years it does not work out and your partner breaks up with you. You can't accept it. It is more than a calamity. It is unthinkable. The obsession is born to get him/her back. This is a typical example: A woman had underbelly problems. Some warts were removed. When she was 17 she started a relationship with John. When she was 23, John decided to live with another woman. Despite of that she kept on seeing him regularly having sex with him hoping he would finally choose for her. For four years long she tried to win him back with all her manipulations. Sure she was good looking. When she finally realized it didn't make any sense, she made a firm decision to break up for good. It felt like finishing her childhood. She got another lover, much younger than she, but she was unsure whether she really loved him. She simply did not know. Do I love him or not? He loved her very much, taking her out, showing her places and doing his utter best to comfort her. But something was missing. She did not dare to tell him. So she continued the relationship. Alice was suffering her Pluto in the eighth house problem from both sides. First she experienced an obsessive love for somebody who did not want her. Later she had a love affair with someone she actually did not want.

The essence of Pluto in the eighth house is the purity of your love. Do you want a man for unconditional love or do you want a man because your children need a daddy? Or: what would you do when you are a teacher and you fall obsessively in love with one of your pupils?

Some don't start a relationship because they doubt their purity of love. "Why do I love her? Is this love?" they ask themselves and they don't know it anymore. The more they question themselves the less the know. The more they think about it the more they don't know what that is 'love'. By this insecurity they let it be. The most difficult situation occurs when you first think you love somebody and later not anymore. They find it awful hard to handle this change.

For natives with Pluto in the eighth house sex is a transformative force. Sex makes you high. With sex you experience the ultimate togetherness. Sex force is 'too big to handle'. This power gets you out of control pushing you over all your limits. That is queer so you hold back. They are emotionally locked up and wait for being opened. It would be a good idea to go to a tantric teacher with your spouse.

What can happen to women with Pluto in the eighth house is that a man is interested in you but he does not come to the point. You don't love him but you want to help him in his problem. He keeps on approaching you and you keep him on the line because you want to find out his secret and straighten him out. It is making you crazy and actually you hate him. Still you don't say: "Bug off! Hit the road and don't come back no more!" Instead you try to be his therapist. How nice.

Natives with Pluto in the eighth house have an ambiguity in their commitment. By your over commitment you can't see the situation clearly. First you do what you can to be supportive. Suddenly by some event you give up. You are disappointed. See, that is the way he is (bad) you conclude and you turn your back. You are emotionally hurt but you don't realize it. See, he is not to be trusted. You not only turn your back but you turn against him. You'll teach him a lesson. Your love has changed into hate. You flip sides and the other feels betrayed. This can happen when you are a teacher. Your pupils are dear to you. But there is one student, he simply is not good in your eyes. He is a lazy bum, a mischievous brat or whatever. You think he is just like that. Although you gave up all hopes he would change you start picking on him to make him change. You are projecting your fear for all the evils in the world on that pupil. A hopeless emotional conflict is born. This also might happen to your child. If he is not what you thought he was, you are disappointed and even mad. When he does something wrong and gets in problems with the authorities (justice) or otherwise in a bad situation you get emotional and tend to blame him. That's no help. You are too closely associated if though you yourself did it and will get the blame for it. Not even your spouse is able to point out to you out you are being unreasonable.

When you are a therapist you might get afraid for the anger of your client. You meet your own fears in your client. You might get obsessively afraid he is going to kill someone or you even. You start to emphasis he should not do that. He never intended to do so and gets emotional because you think he is like that. Beware of your own part in the story. It is more likely this happens when you are not a therapist. You get in trouble with someone because you accuse hem and after all were our fears not justified.

Natives with Pluto in the eighth house get completely out

of line when a child is born or somebody dies. Men don't know how to behave when a child is born. Nervous as a rat they only get in the way and are a problem themselves. They are panicky. They run away. They don't show up. They behave like a nut doing everything wrong causing a post-natal depression in their wives. This can cause serious damage to their relationship. She will remember how he behaved during those critical moments. And you are not able to explain what had got into you. Women worry a lot when they are pregnant. All kinds of worries.

Also when somebody dies they overreact. They are inconsolable. They don't stop sobbing. For years they mourn especially when someone of the family or another dear one died. You might even get physically sick laying in your bed not able to do anything like you have died yourself. You miss the deceased. He/she is talking to you. When you think of him you get all kind of pains. It is the Pluto in the eighth house problem of cutting the ties. It really is like he is still there. It is making you crazy. It helps you to crack Pluto to get a deeper consciousness about the mystery of life and death. The deceased one is back home, where he came from. This excessive sadness is not necessary.

Some natives with Pluto in the eighth house have to deal with death all their life. That is special karma. At a young age one after the other deceases. I remember a women I coached: Her father died of leukemia when she was a teenager. Her first boyfriend committed suicide. Her second boyfriend died in a car crash after she made it out. Since then she did not dare to relate anymore. When she was 30 her older brother died of cancer on the age of 33. She always admired her older brother. When he died she had an aching hollow feeling in her stomach for years. When she was telling me her story she wiped away her tears making a cynical joke: "Don't relate with me. You won't survive it."

Of course she understood her brother was better off up in heaven out of his pains but still she had that hollow feeling.

Some natives with Pluto in the eighth house are obsessively worried something will happen to their children. They are over concerned and protect their children against all kinds of dangers. That is a problem for those children because they are not free. Constantly Mama is watching/controlling them. It might be that in a past life her entire family was murdered.

Cracking Pluto in the eighth house means a relaxation on your emotions and how you relate. Before you either loved someone or you despised/hated him. When transiting Pluto enters the eleventh house your love will be transformed into (cosmic) friendship. The sharp edges of your emotions will soften up. Your lover becomes a friend, your best friend, your trustee and if possible your twin soul. You learn to keep distance without losing your emotions. This way you become more direct and to the point. When your marriage is in a deadlock you face the problem and name it. During cracking Pluto you cannot hold in or keep silent anymore. All the time you hoped for a change but it did not happen. Now it is an absolute must. You forgive the shortcomings of your partner. Together you sort out how things could have grown that bad, how you two became strangers to each other. And you take the consequences. Either you come together again or you split with no hard feelings. Often it is a problem that your spouse is completely taken by surprise. He/she was unaware of it and does not understand. Your spouse might be desperate. You always were her/his security. It is emotionally hard to see that happen. The realm of your spouse is too different to bridge. But you have to be honest with yourself and the situation. Surprisingly how many natives still stay together knowing this.

For the ones who never dared to relate cracking Pluto in the eighth house is a getting back your passion. Suddenly you obsessively fall in love with someone. It happens to you. You can't help it. Even when you are fifty five or older this can happen to you. For decennia you ran away from it. It is a tantric wakening up. It means you face all the beginners problems explained above. But by that time transformation has become your power so within a few months you get through it. It might be this love becomes a drama but still you have gone through your evolution.

The icy cold moneygrubbers will find out during cracking Pluto that nobody loves them. It might be our wife will run away hurting you where she can when you are forty. She takes off with another. She will tell you she found out she is lesbian and prefers her new girlfriend. Conservative as you are you are hurt deep into your bones. Moreover it will cost you money. Divorce is a costly affair. The same happens in your social life. Everybody turns his back on you because of money conflicts. At the end you are completely alone. If you pretend not to care you never crack Pluto.

Natives with Pluto in the eighth house have great problems to face in a changed situation. Nothing stays the same in this world, also not your love. You know you can't stay in passion all your life. It alters, not for the good neither for the bad. It just alters. Understanding and responding to the changes is hard. But once natives with Pluto in the eighth house get into the flow of change they cannot be stopped anymore. The eighth house is the transformation house and Pluto is power. So once they face their emotional problems they run to five therapists and six healers at the same time and fix it. Within a few weeks they are fully transformed.

Basically cracking Pluto is about solving the ambiguity between caring and not caring at all, between over-concern and distance. Therapists with Pluto in the eighth house get into their power after cracking Pluto. Before that they should be very careful being a therapist. It means you show more respect for the evolution of your client. You realize it is impossible to change somebody in one day. You are less demanding. If there is no progress you see it in perspective without turning your back. You keep your loving feeling despite all.

Cracking Pluto in the eighth house means you learn when your concern is wanted or not. You become less manipulative and more direct. It means a relaxation in dealing with people When they don't want you or your concern it is no problem.

Pluto in the ninth house

Natives with Pluto in the ninth house suffer a drive and a fear to live the right way. When issues about ideology, religion and philosophy pop up an enormous stress rises up 'too big to handle'. You like to discuss but when you can't win the discussion you block and you get mad. The problem is insecurity. How do you know for sure whether something is right (true) or not. You seek for an absolute vision about life. You expect someone else to present it to you and you get upset when it is not consistent or does not match. But you hold in and pretend to agree because you don't know or dare to tackle it. Especially when authorities are at stake you pretend to be a decent obedient citizen but at the same time a potential revolutionary is hiding within you. The split is: you are afraid of judge mentalism and you are judgmental yourself.

The mortal fear surrounding ideological issues stems from past lives. In those days you were prosecuted and tortured to death for your believe. Or even worse you were a prosecutor yourself although you knew deep in your heart that what you did was not right. But if you didn't you would have been tortured yourself. Or you were forced to enhance a religion, a believe, you did not agree with. Your entire life was pestered by this belief. Out of fear for punishment and torture you adapted. Could be you were indeed brainwashed. In this life you don't want any brainwashing anymore. No more self-renunciation. You want to live by your own convictions. That is the drive. Doing so you cope with tremendous fears. It all had to do with religious fanaticism in past lives. That is the pest. Not only for the individual but in the history of mankind. I also recorded a Pluto in the ninth house past life dealing with a preacher man in the 16th century. He died in disillusion for the unthankful task of being a spiritual leader. It was too lonely. *He could not do any concessions.*

When children with Pluto in the ninth house get criticized they feel intimidated. They take the family rules very seriously and as absolute. Those rules are based on some belief. The child loses the discussion which feels like a crucifixion. He has to adapt. That is how it ought to be and nothing else. Daddy is always right. The same happens in school. A blind obedience to authorities is born. A fear sets in against expressing original ideas. Capital punishment is waiting for you so you hold in. It might be the parents are nice and the family rules are not that bad. But if the parents are unreasonable and their rules are dumb it later becomes very hard to get rid of this indoctrination. Even when you are an adult your parents try to impose their wicked ideas on you. This struggle will continue until you crack Pluto.

Natives with Pluto in the ninth house love philosophic treatments about good and bad, how you should live and the basic decisions in life. The problem is that they look for the absolute truth. They are easily swayed by a book or a person who pretend to have the higher knowledge, especially when this person is of high rank. When they meet someone with another vision they get nervous. Getting into a discussion they easily get upset. Confronted with some kind of theory which is not theirs they can't find the words. Only days later you find the counter argument. But then it is too late. You already agreed. The other way around: They get hypnotized by a theory and forget about the overall picture. They get tunneled in. It goes like this: You meet someone who tells you something. You are interested and after a talk you agree. It becomes your belief. You keep on thinking about it and you talk around. Years later you find out it is not true. The Plutonic reaction sets in: you get mad. You start to dislike if not hate that person and all who think that way.

When it comes to discussions the Plutonic problem sets in. Either you win the discussion and 'they' agree with you. You like to be a teacher (priest) and to explain how the matter stands. No problem. But when 'they' don't agree then a problem arises, especially with a person who is dear to you or at work. Somehow by reason of some irrational stress natives with Pluto in the ninth house can't win the discussion (third house). They don't dare to have a sharp tongue. A weak 'not true' comes out of their mouth and then they keep silent. The split is: You are afraid to be considered a dissident and at the same time you are afraid of dissidents. A dissident is someone who does not think right. The fear of being excommunicated eventually beats the freedom of speech. It is very hard to develop your own consistent theory. You don't do that in a minute. Every time you try you get stuck and you have to go back on your word. You get overruled again, again and again. If you avoid the discussion you get cornered in too. It seems to be a catch 22. The thing is that natives with Pluto in the 9th house can get very angry when someone disagrees with them and they can't win the discussion. They start a hidden battle against people who don't think right.
Years ago when I published my first book a group of astrologers wrote a recension showing they did not really understand it. I contacted them but they were stubborn. A me-

diator, not the first one, called me up. She had Pluto in the ninth house. She wanted to mediate. Patiently she listened to all my arguments. She fully agreed and would hand over the message in their next meeting. I had the feeling she completely understood me. A week later she called me up. She had put all my arguments on the table and a tough discussion took place. She switched. I asked for their arguments. I gave my comments and after half an hour she had nothing to bring in anymore and she switched again. "Well," she said, "I will give you their telephone number so you can sort it out together." Very wise, by this she cracked her Pluto. I called that number and my defense was published. She was wiser than I thought. Later she began her own political party. But also this was temporary.

If the fear wins and the adoption is complete there is a chance you get narrow minded. You live like you are told to live. You need a book, a theory, to hold onto. This theory might be accompanied by a broad set of rules. In the incessant course of influencing and being influenced they long for a firm stand. So you go to the highest authority for an answer: a professor. The professor thinks deeply and answers your question. "Thank you," you respond, "now I know". Now you know and you stick to it. If you hear about another contradicting life philosophy you get confused. This confusion has no words but it comes in deeply and is scary. There are some people who don't think right. The blaming finger is pointed. It is threatening because if that is true all your walls tumble down. The basis of your life is wiped out. Even worse it means you were wrong all your life. That cannot be. Suppose you are raised catholic. A man comes up telling you about reincarnation. This is not according to the catholic belief. You conclude that this man must be the devil himself. Natives with Pluto in the ninth house need a philosophy as a basis for their life. The next step is to become narrow minded. You stick toward your own cultural group, your kind of people, and the one who thinks differently is out. All in the dark, you are not open about it.

If the power wins and you stand for your own point of view. Like a preacher you try to convince everybody. You try to from a group that shares your concepts. If you succeed it will be temporarily until the cracking of Pluto. But mostly you find that you get crushed in the discussion. You adapt, you have got to, but under protest. Deep inside you know how it is but ..... you can't explain it. You are holding in and at the same time you keep on worrying. Now and then you try to make a stand for some of your own standpoints but you don't get recognition. You hear them say: "You really got it wrong. If you stubbornly believe in what you say then we can't be friends anymore." So you do adapt but the brainwashing is not total. You keep on doubting. You are not openly protesting but keep it hidden by the way you dress, by symbols and by supporting those who do better in the discussion. Some natives with Pluto in the ninth house become a gadfly undermining all theories. Simultaneously they are brewing on the allover vision of life but as long as it is not fully worked out (it never will) you don't dare to present it. When you get tackled you don't know what to say anymore. You lose your tongue realizing every word you say will make it worse. So you shut up and keep quiet. It is like your brain gets paralyzed. It becomes empty. There is nothing anymore. You are lost. It is over. Silence remains. Even going underground is not an option. It is like dying.

In the dawning of the age of Aquarius the Pisces religious

rule will be changed into political rule. Nowadays you are not anymore Catholic, Calvinist, Lutheran, Orthodox or heathen. You are liberal, republican, democrat, unionist or green. That is how you get caged in. Natives with Pluto in the ninth house are extremely sensitive about this. When they are political engaged they identify themselves with a political philosophy. It is very dear to them. As long as you have not cracked Pluto this philosophy is almost always connected with the establishment out of safety reasons. In my generation there was a general communist fear called 'the cold war syndrome'. Behind every tree a communistic anarchist was hiding, sabotaging the society. Those are the basic fears of Pluto in the ninth house. Nowadays the general threat is the Muslim radical. In the year 50 AD all astrologers were banned from Rome because of their poisonous influence on the society. One of my astrology students went to the doctor. Besides Pluto she had a bunch of other planets in the ninth house. To Ebertin her physical problems all pointed to Pluto. She told the doctor everything including that she was following my course. The doctor told her she should not go to my course anymore and should not read those difficult books. It would only confuse her. She should care for her children and read pulp novels and not think too much. She called me up to unsubscribe to my course. I convinced (!) her to stay. The next meeting she showed me her new pulp novel, a heavy and thick book about (fiction) a young Palestinian boy in the middle of the Jewish–Arabian conflict. I did not tell her that the doctor clearly explained to her not to read those difficult books. I only laughed. A man with Pluto in the ninth house told me he had to work together with a man who was openly a communist. In the beginning he was very nervous dealing with him. But after a few months he found out this man was very nice. What a release. He was 35 years old and cracking his Pluto. He tried to explain me it does not really matter what your believe is as long as your heart is on the right side.

Some natives with Pluto in the ninth house seemingly live by the rules but they have a second life in which they live by their own rules. This can lead to serious conflicts culminating in a catastrophe during cracking Pluto. The preacher man in the 16th century mentioned above was born with a hate against the materialistic/capitalistic world he was born in. He had an ordinary job but he was cheating the bankers in loaning a lot of money from all different sides and playing the big spender for his friends and family. At the age of 36 he fell through the bucket confronted with a debt he never could pay off. To his surprise he was not executed but an arrangement was found. He had as his punishment to work hard for a few years for very little money and then he was free. Doing sessions with me, this past life hatred came out. Note: he was clever enough to fool the bankers. Another bright man with Pluto in the ninth house with a master's degree in psychology got a job in a company doing professional talent tests. He had to do these tests according to the philosophy of the company. Secretly he was using his own much better way of testing. When it came out he was fired on the spot. Red hot mad he was. He always had excellent results!

The big problem of natives with Pluto in the ninth house is: how do you know for sure whether something is true or not. First your parents told you the truth. But it was nonsense. Then at school the professors tried to tell you the truth. But they all disagreed. Nobody is able to tell you. So you have to do it yourself. But how do you prove something is true or not. If you cannot prove it, it does not mean it is not true. The stress is that if you think something is true and later on it appears not to be true then you have the illusion that you will be hanged. And indeed, in a past life this might have happened. So, 'what do you believe?' is the pressed question of natives with Pluto in the ninth house.

Natives with Pluto in the ninth house face the problem of designing a life philosophy for themselves. From the beginning they want to redefine it. Deep inside they know but they can't put it into words. Each time they try they get stuck. It is even comical how easily they are tackled. But for them it is deadly serious. If you ask them if they really know what they are talking about their eyes start to twinkle. "Yes, deep inside I know but now it is too much to explain all at once. You just wait until I publish my book." But they never finish that book. If you ask them why they haven't published their book they answer that they are afraid that if it gets too big the whole world will jump on them. OK, that's true. I know. But if you write a sound book you will also be approached by supporters. After they have cracked Pluto most lose their drive to write that book. They start writing articles instead.

With cracking Pluto in the ninth house the search for the truth really begins. You start to read books. Before you only read books that you were told to read. Now you read them all. Natives with Pluto in the ninth house have the ability to read five books, 450 pages each, in one week and the most difficult ones too. A tremendous amount of energy gets freed. They follow philosophical courses too: three at the same time. The search for the truth can be compared with the myth of the search for the holy grail. Somewhere on earth a golden bowl is hidden containing the truth.

The big mistake the middle aged knights made was they thought this bowl was material. Go to a holy place, dig in the ground and you'll find it. Or it might be hidden in a castle, or somewhere in the bushes of a far-away land, in a book or in the womb of a woman, or at the top of a high mountain. Wherever the knights of the holy grail went, they could not find it. They searched the truth outside. The ones who did survive, like Percival, found out the holy grail is not material. It is in your own heart. That is how it goes with Pluto in the ninth house. First you expect someone else to tell you the truth until you have heard so many truths, you have to make your own synthesis. During cracking Pluto in the ninth house you begin to understand the higher truth. You open up to the fact that there are several truths. There is no absolute truth.

Cracking Pluto means you dare to go for your own point of view, your own truth ..... openly. Making up your mind you first begin with a sound study of the matter. When you sorted it all out you enter the discussion. You say: "Listen, I red so much of this stuff I know all the points of view. To me this is the big line that it is all about." You unfold your own doctrine, your own creation, your own truth, your own opinion about the case without citing a holy professor or something like that. And you find out they go for it. You discover the power of your higher mind. Doing so you get stronger and stronger. You don't care so much about a general doctrine. You become practical. You start to write articles about specific issues. You subscribe to committees: a political committee, research committees, an astrology committee, education committees, committees of whatever matter people disagree on. Natives with Pluto in the ninth house have a message. The danger is not to fall back in absolutism: my vision is the best. Cracking Pluto is a daily thing. Basically there is no difference between Muslims, Christians, Buddhists, left or right wing politicians or classical or esoteric astrology. We all want a better world, don't we. What? No? Hm. Plutonic silence.

When you crack Pluto in the ninth house you are no follower anymore. Suppose you followed some astrology courses and you are enthusiastic about it. You don't become just a member of an astrology group. You create your own group with your own synthesis based on your own research. If you go into politics you create your own political party or unit. The karmic object is not to be killed this time. Once they transformed this karma they usually stop being a politician.

Cracking Pluto in the ninth house means you let go of all your fears and go for it. A power is released stronger than diamond to discover, to connect, to talk, to persuade, to be persuaded and to get it all clear. It is not for the fun. It is obligatory. If you don't you might get sick.

When you crack Pluto in the ninth house a release and tolerance is created towards belief systems. You don't panic anymore when someone is bothering you with their theories. You don't lose your head and you keep calm when someone is telling you tales. You have your truth and that's it. That is your inner certainty based on experience. You decide to live according to your own standards no matter what. No more fancy discussions. You live by your belief instead of preaching it. Of course you can explain it too. It means you make a shift in your connections. You disconnect yourself from everyone who tries to impose a rule on you. When Pluto was transiting the eleventh house there was a tension and push to live by the rules of the major majority. With transiting Pluto in the twelfth house you dissolve in All consciousness freeing you from this yoke.

You get an overall conception telling you all this dogmatism is of no use. It might be you go abroad and find your luck somewhere else where it is possible to live your own way. For example the psychologist doing the professional talent tests mentioned above cracked his Pluto in the ninth house by going abroad to another part of the country to start his own practice as professional talent researcher own style. He had good results, didn't he.

During cracking Pluto in the ninth house you somehow will be asked for your vision. For example at your work there is a grand discussion about the company policy, the future plans and how to grow further. The highest CEO invites you personally to hear your ideas. Before you always tried to avoid a conflict by choosing for both sides. Now it is impossible and you have to come with your standpoint. If you do so and of course you have thought about it a lot, you will see your view is accepted. If you stay calm and frankly explain what you think you find out there is no problem. You will find each other. During cracking Pluto in the ninth house the fear concerning belief systems is transformed into a joy and commitment to it. You rediscover your power, your power of persuasion. Real persuasion is about content.

The essence of cracking Pluto in the ninth house is to stand for your vision. Living together or working for someone with another vision is in the long run impossible. You detach from those people. Before cracking Pluto you were not able to do so. Always you submitted yourself to someone else's vision. By the time of cracking Pluto the cosmos challenges you one way or another to stand for your vision in public. Once you do that you discover your power. It does not come out of the blue. All your life you have been thinking about this stuff. You know about all possible visions on earth. You know what you are talking about. Once you throw away your fears your golden treasure will be freed: your philosophical insight. You don't become a spiritual leader. You stay true to your own vision without being a missionary. You only give your vision when you are asked to.

After cracking Pluto in the ninth house you are freer in your thinking. It is easier to accept different viewpoints. As the time goes by you become freer and freer to express your ideas. A myriad of ideas are released for the benefit of mankind and your own too. When transiting Pluto enters the first house all the floodgates will be opened ...... and you might become an example for others. In this period it is the challenge to stay modest and not to become an all knowing dictator. Remember to crack Pluto daily.

Pluto in the tenth house

Natives with Pluto in the tenth house suffer a basic fear of being open. You are afraid of not being liked. So you smile and play it cool. Your popularity is all importance. Natives with Pluto in the tenth house seem to be nice and cool but when you get to know them they ain't (excuse me: are not) …… until they cracked Pluto. When it comes down to it your social position, career and reputation prevails above friendship. Basically natives with Pluto in the tenth house are power freaks. In what you say or do you always calculate the consequences. You are not easy to negotiate with but when you agree you are very loyal. The split is: you want to be the boss but you always feel there is a super boss above you. There is a fear and adoration for people of power, of high position.

The past life memories of natives with Pluto in the tenth house revolve around having a high position with a catastrophically bad end. Classical: You were a good (political) leader of a tribe or sect, hanged by your opponents. Or: You were a big minister of state business and you became the center of a scandal. Or even worse: to prevent being the victim of a scandal you bribed, intrigued and betrayed. A considerable amount of natives with Pluto in the tenth house still feel guilty for the wrong doings they did in their high position in a past life. You had to do it. If not you would be hanged yourself. You had to be cruel to get respect. It is all about Machiavelli. Feelings are of no importance. Power is impersonal. There is no room for personal affection. The paradox is: you hate it but you think you can't get around it.

Another past life pain of Pluto in the tenth house is: It is lonely at the top. Once you got that position you became a prisoner of your position. Resigning was impossible. I have witnesses several past life of natives with Pluto in the tenth house being a priest(ess) in the old Inca time controlling the population with their thinking power through their third eye, constructing a telepathic television everyone had to obey. In one case he himself was locked up alone in the temple with all his tools of power doing the rituals in strict control. He was unhappy all his life.

The power of natives with Pluto in the tenth house is their sense of power. From past life experiences they know the structures of power. They know what it is. They are great organizers. But there is a fear to be overpowered and a push to control the situation. It is hard to be casual and informal. There is always a snag somewhere ….. They are afraid to be tackled. They are great tacklers themselves. It is to tackle or be tackled.

Natives with Pluto in the tenth house have a problem with being true to themselves. You don't say and do what you really want. You need the permission of someone placed above you. You need clear rules so nobody can blame you afterwards. Not your own heart but the rules and the schedules are the final authority. If an authority tells you to do something you think you'll get shot when you don't. Don't you challenge the authorities. If you have to make a decision by yourself and the choice is free the problem starts. Since you don't dare to push yourself as an authority (this is what I want) you conjure up another authority. Someone who told you so. This is stuck deep in your mind and when you meet opposition you panic. It is the problem of hiding behind a fake authority.

A small minority of natives with Pluto in the tenth house revolt. They get sick of obediently saying 'yes sir' and 'thy will be done'. Inside they are thinking inside: 'fuck you' and 'I won't'. Still they have to do it. So, they become radical. But even then, ….. they are not free. It is reactive.

The power struggle begins in your childhood with a grand collapse with the boss of the family: the father. You must know how many natives with Pluto in the tenth house I did sessions with to go over the terrible fight with their father. The fight to be your own authority starts with your father. Often natives with Pluto in the tenth house have a very authoritarian father, a jerk, a simple minded redneck intimidating and menacing in all ways. Only sometimes it is the mother. Sometimes the whole family is a member of some sort of extremist sect or belief (for example a motor club) they have to submit to. In the hectic confrontation about the do's and don'ts and how to behave the child loses. They have to do things they don't like and if not ….. they get a pack of beatings they remember for the rest of their life. They were a big boss in a past life and now they are under the thumb of a big boss, their father. As an astrologer you just ask how bad it was and you get your stories. So they become very obedient, teacher's pet. A child with Pluto in the tenth house easily feels obligated. They make sure to do well in school because the higher your degree the higher your status. It looks nicer than it is. A client being a scientific researcher confessed to me: Her life had been one big exam hell.

Sometimes a native with Pluto in the tenth house is forced to stay longer at their parents' home than usual. Taken hostage by the family out of some mental obligation. They had to stay having to care for ..... More often they run away from home young, escaping family rule. Sometimes they marry to escape their family.

Natives with Pluto in the tenth house present themselves as nicer than they are. They make good public relations managers. They play the social game perfectly well making sure they are liked. Secretly they know they are a prisoner of good behavior. They keep on smiling and don't dare to say what they really think. Their laugh is nervous. Don't make enemies. In advance they dig in against every accusation possible. To be cool they present themselves to be modern and broad minded but if a new idea fails they make sure they are not the target of blame. Not me. I have nothing to do with it.

Having Pluto in the tenth house in your astrology chart means there is a super tension between your social standing and your private life. Social standing is top priority and private life hardly exists. They go for a career. The top is ..... status and money. They go for the board of directors. They go for a company with status: A university, a famous lawyers' office, a fancy investors association, you name it. They don't become an ordinary doctor, they specialize in psychiatry. Next they work for justice deciding which suicidal or criminal should be locked up for safety reasons. I never met an uneducated against all odds self-made millionaire having Pluto in the tenth house. No, they make a career in a classified organization. If they have their own company, for example as a computer specialist, they have prestigious clients. They love to be a member of important committees. They want to be in the deciding position but they always need someone placed above them for safety reasons. If they get in trouble they can always hide behind this (fake) authority. They don't perform themselves. They sit in a chair telling others how to perform.

Natives with Pluto in the tenth house push themselves to the limit. Nothing less but the top. They are walking on their toes. They like to show off that they have got it made. They are perfectly dressed using a bit too much make-up. They want respect. They look up at high officials. They want to be a high official themselves. If they are not they pretend they are. As long as they have not cracked Pluto they always need an authority to tell them what to do. They are not the professor but a member of his staff. Their work is important, pushing them to the edge of exhaustion for an international breakthrough. They are afraid to underperform. They need the recognition of someone placed above them, the professor, the board of directors. *Deep inside they need the permission of someone placed above them.* It can also go this way: Suppose you are a woman and your family did not want to support your education (a typical Pluto in the tenth house frustration). At a young age you left home and became a secretary to make some bread. Pretty soon you were promoted to be the secretary of the director, the highest chief. At the end it is you who are the decision maker in the company because of your magic influence on the boss. He is like wax in your hands.

Having a partnership with someone with Pluto in the tenth house means occasional tough confrontations about the line to be followed. It is all about having the last word. Beware to turn down their proposals. They take it personally. A battery of dirty tricks will be pulled on you. They set up all their connections to step on you. Pluto in the tenth house all is all about prestige. They easily feel attacked. Beware for their reprisals. They can get really nasty. Trembling tyrants are dangerous. A silly argument becomes the battle of the ages. Not cool at all.

10% to 20% of the natives, mostly women, with Pluto in the tenth house become idealists. They don't want to slime and lick above. They want to make the world a better place. They join an alternative group having their own lifestyle, promoting this lifestyle as the way to be. This is a repetition of a past life when they were the leader of a sect. Again they are a leader. This archetype has to be lived out fully until the cracking of Pluto. They volunteer in community work. They become a neighborhood-star. Living in a deprived neighborhood they join environmental committees. Pretty soon they become the chairman and the big organizer. The power of Pluto in the tenth house is the power to organize. They organize conferences, manifestations, soup kitchens, educational courses, and promotional campaigns. Everybody looks up to them. They neglect their private life for the holy goal of making the world a better place. But the same thing occurs when they should have chosen for the other side: they push themselves too hard, standing on their toes for their holy task, making a statue out of themselves. In the end there is no personal touch anymore.

Often natives with Pluto in the tenth house have an expression on their face which is not real. They show an impersonal face about how you should be. Sick or ill, no matter what, I have got to go to my job. No matter how awful I feel, I have to smile and look happy. This is horrible, especially for the natives themselves. In the long run you cannot hold it up. At home they grouch and at work they keep up appearances. Finally an explosion follows, a big argument about how you want things to be done, and it is over. A lot of irritation builds up and in time releases. When it is that far it will not stay with one argument. This can happen during cracking Pluto or this happens all the time before cracking Pluto. The fear of Pluto in the tenth house is a spiritual fear to be wrong. A fear of disapproval. A fear to glide off the social ladder, to go down. People might think wicked things about you. Once you've lost their respect they step on you, is the thought. So you cover yourself up in advance.

During cracking Pluto the crisis sets in. You cannot or will not fulfill all the expectations anymore. You have the feeling not to get back enough in turn. Emotionally you did not get the credits. It's lonely at the top. You are not happy. You don't have real friends, only business associates. The feeling grows of a need for a change. You don't want to play your social role anymore. Too long you were standing on your toes to reach the top. Either you find your final adversary who tackles you or you want to quit yourself. You back up and find a way of living so as not to have to push yourself that hard anymore. You become human again. When transiting Pluto enters the first house squaring your natal Pluto it often happens that you get tired, physically worn out. You realize you don't feel well this way. Something must change. The Plutonic transformation concerns your attitude in your job and in your private life. The latter becomes more important. They all look up to you and you long for real affection. Either it goes easy and you decide for yourself to step back. The disgust against all the formalities passes the limit and you start another life. Suppose you were always the second man executing the commands from above you quit this role. Suppose you was the neighborhood-star you quit it too. Not my piece of cake anymore. You apply for a job, less in status and stress. This way a lot of time will be freed for yourself.

It might go the hard way. A latent conflict flares up or an existing conflict comes to a climax. This conflict is either won or lost. There is no middle way. Either he goes or you go. It might be you win and you become the big professor yourself as a next step in the social ladder. Now you have the chance to set out your own megalomania lines. Now you are the first man. Then the stress not to underperform only becomes worse and you find your Waterloo later. You'll for sure get fatigue phenomena. It will not last. Suppose you 'lose' and you go. It feels like dying. Finally they got you out. "Congratulations!" you say to your opponents. How frustrating. Cracking Pluto means you realize it is actually your win. It is not your problem anymore. Now you can aim for the positive things in life.

The result of cracking Pluto in the tenth house is that you find work and a social life in another, nicer, department. More time is freed for your personal life. You decide to live on a lower gear and to be more easy going. No more of all those power games. No more standing on your toes. You step back on the social ladder and more time is freed to do the things you love and to be with people you love instead of getting around with all those competitors.

Cracking Pluto in the tenth house is like a grand finale. Cosmically it was no way of living. You were stuck in your work. At the end your system and network collide. If not described as above you get a mysterious sickness forcing you to step out. Or you continue your job, being tackled and pushed away, with an attitude not to care anymore and doing nothing extra for no bonus. This is a spiritual death. You better step out.

But having stepped out a new problem pops up. It is hard

to be casual, relaxed, easy going, cozy or familiar whatever the word is. You never knew what that was. The feeling of togetherness was lost. It is hard to feel comfortable being together. The basic distrust of being trapped and used is hard to get rid of and ruins the feeling of togetherness. If there is no talking about big business anymore where should be talked about then at least. This leaves you with a lonely feeling. If you are not important anymore what are you then. But you are talking to friends. I hear you thinking: "Friends? What's that?" That is a non-enemy. The problem is not to get sucked into power games anymore. It takes a while, for this consciousness fully saturated your soul.

During cracking Pluto in the tenth house you experience a change in attitude. First you were a hot shot whose decisions were of all importance. Now you are an ordinary man which gives you the freedom to be yourself. Of course you still continue advising and organizing. That is the power of Pluto in the tenth house. But it is not of overall importance anymore. First they liked you because you were important and now they like you because they really do. They like your presence with nothing to gain or to lose. No matter how well you know to organize. The switch is a deep mental transformation into modesty and love for the ordinary things of life. It is not something you can fake. People feel it. As long as you don't make that switch there is no real togetherness. It means a change in social life. You will meet new people to make this possible. A change in job means you choose for the good atmosphere instead of prestige. No more crisis management. This way organizing becomes fun.

I met a millionaire asking me if the time was right to legalize his Swiss bank account. He had already bought a motorcycle to replace his Cadillac. His 40 year old girl-friend loved to sit behind. That is what he liked. I told him: legalize and go on your motorcycle without worries. Transiting Pluto in the first house means you follow your instincts. I met another 40 year old millionaire whose hedge fund went bankrupt. He wanted to start a new software house developing programs for the insurance business. He planned to start with two highly qualified trustees to grow a 150 employees company in two years. I told him it would not work out but he did not want to hear that.

Some natives with Pluto in the tenth house crack their Pluto when they are pensioned. They have had a fantastic career. They have a beautiful mansion, a loving wife and the kids are doing well. Now that they are pensioned they have no projects anymore. They have nothing to do. They are empty handed. It is like a black hole. The last thing you should do is starting a new project like you always did. Instead you should enjoy your riches (transiting Pluto in the second house). Amazing how hard that is. You should keep on organizing though. That's the power of Pluto in the tenth house.

Cracking Pluto in the tenth house is all about softening up. That is no weakness. On the contrary it is strength. You have got the experience and are strong enough to be soft. No way softening up means you'll be abused. It is honesty to yourself. In this time you need people to philosophize with what to do with your life. It is possible your spouse will be of big help. Your interest is her/his interest. Go on vacation, on a world trip. It is something to organize. You'll find new people with refreshing ideas. People without a hidden agenda. In this process a new personality is born, a person without worries.

Pluto in the eleventh house

Natives with Pluto in the eleventh house are detached from the group by an irrational fear. This fear creeps in when you join an organization or go to meetings. Also at parties and all kinds of mass activities with large groups of people. They are afraid the crowd will turn against them. They have an ambiguous attitude towards politics. The split is: they are very committed to politics and the faith of the community. It is always on their mind. But they hate the way it goes. Deep in their heart they are egalitarian and want the good for all. They fear dictatorship and peer pressure. By self-fulfilling prophecy it happens. A lot of natives with Pluto in the eleventh house get into problems with institutions. Some natives with Pluto in the eleventh house are born with a hopeless 'alone against the mafia' feeling. They have a strong commitment to the society. At the same time they are afraid.

Natives with Pluto in the eleventh house have bad past life memories related to loyalty, faith and politics. The bond you had was brutally broken. Your own people turned against you. You were made a public culprit and the mob lynched you. You were the chief of a tribe and the younger generation dethroned you. A lot of times inequality of justice is the theme. You were a rich 19th century charity woman caring for the poor but killed by the mafia. Another example: He was born in the Ukraine. In the 1930's he was about twenty years old joining meetings discussing the political situation. In one of those meetings they decided to set fire to a community house in a village in the region. He knew that village, the community house and the woman counselling over there. He respected her very much. Next night they parted to commit the crime. Along the way he started protesting: "Hey guys, we should not do this. We can't do that." But they did not want to hear him and they said: "Ok, if you don't want to join us you can just wait outside the village. We are going to do it anyway." He waited outside the village. He saw fire lighting up. The guys came back and without any warning knocked him down and kicked him to death with their big black boots. Next he was born with Pluto in the eleventh house. I recorded a Pluto in the eleventh house past life of somebody who was set up to assassinate a political leader. He did that because he was poor and miserable and was bribed by beautiful promises.

Another reason of being born with Pluto in the eleventh house is having lived a life in choking social control. You were born as a woman in a Victorian culture where literally nothing was allowed except for drinking your tea the right way. Or you were born in a secret cult family. Once you stepped out they knew where to find you. Many European natives with Pluto in the eleventh house have memories of the Nazi time. Without any warning the uniformed soldiers came and deported you to their torture place. In general natives with Pluto in the eleventh house fear the power of mobs, uniformed or not.

Natives with Pluto in the eleventh house have a high social consciousness and at the same time they behave anti-socially. They immediately feel the power structures in a group. The boss kicks the underboss, the underboss kicks his subordinates and the subordinates collectively point their finger at you, the lowest in rank. They don't want to belong to one group. They belong to many groups. If one group turns against you, you still have another group to go to. Basically someone with Pluto in the eleventh house is a loving revolutionary who does not dare to be. They have idealistic ideas but get tensed up talking about it or living by it. They fear the irrational behavior of the masses. Either they walk away from it or they become ideological fanatics. They feel solidarity with the underdog. But as we all know: that is a dangerous thing.

Children with Pluto in the eleventh house want to join the family and the kids in school. They want to join the crowd. Sometimes they act like the old organizer (past life repetition) creating a majority for an idea. That is how they take the lead. Inevitably a storm breaks out. The kid gets scared. More and more he draws back from the crowd. In large numbers they become awfully silent.
In a pack natives with Pluto in the eleventh house don't dare to show themselves. As long as you are on the sideline it is all right. The moment you have to choose sides you get afraid and out of control. A confusion sets in. Or you behave like a slave and an obedient party voter or you get obnoxious and protesting. They don't really join in. They are observers ready to step out any moment when necessary.

A lot of natives with Pluto in the eleventh house are very trendy. They join the latest music cults, app hypes, places to be and trendy stores. Sometimes they are in the front. They don't initiate. They are followers. They admire the heroes and trendsetters. In the background they are afraid to be thrown out so they exaggerate their admiration to show they are OK. If you find out somebody does not like your club you get mad but you don't show it for survival reasons. A split has set in between 'us' and 'them', all unconscious, hidden and secret.

Natives with Pluto in the eleventh house keep their fear secret. Their fear concerns their own friends. So nobody notices. Nobody knows. Still there is a drive to join a pack. If the drive is bigger than the fear they have a great diversity of connections. They have a friend in one (cultural) group and other friends in other groups. They have a lot of friends. Very clever because when they are thrown out of one group they still have connections in others. It is all about independency. In fact they belong to no one. That is the antisocial part of it. They are lonely. The same counts for friendships. When they observe something wrong their loyalty suddenly stops and the friendship is over. They are good friends but always take into account the risk of being abandoned. They are friends you meet once in a while and not a friend you see daily. You are just one of the many friends they have. They have a lot of connections but don't belong to anybody. If you are an employer and one of your employee's has Pluto in the eleventh house it might be interesting to use his ability in making contacts. They make good salesmen. They make good spies too. They know about the latest trends and who to go to. Somehow they always know the latest gossips. Or even more important: who will be your opponent. So if you want to know about the situation ask them.

The real holding back and silence happens in your circle of friends. Natives with Pluto in the eleventh house never feel really confident at birthday/family parties, reunions or any other get-together. They are the observer. Observing they observe a lot of scary things about what they say, what they think and how they behave. They hold in and play the game. They don't show themselves out of fear to be out of line. Mostly their real thoughts are out of line .... so: don't tell them.

If the fear is bigger than the drive they hide from society. In some cases they grow in complete loneliness. Only the neighbor knows there lives a stranger in that house with the blinded windows. Not that you don't want to take part in the society but you can't. Not able to. If they are in problems they are too scared to ask for help or to go to a lawyer. They hide at home and don't open the door anymore. The basic fear is: a van drives up to your door, two men step out and knock on the door. "Do you have Pluto in the eleventh house?" they ask. Next they drag you away and nobody hears from you again. They live in total isolation. In extreme cases they don't dare to go to the grocery store anymore. They are afraid walking on the street. They suffer agoraphobia. All places with people are weird. A sheer paranoia of the masses. When they hear shouting in a football stadium they shiver and hyperventilate. They feel like outcasts. Once I did a session with a man having these problems. He was a kickboxer and mighty strong. He was poor making money incidentally as an assistant teacher in the gym. Still he was mighty afraid. In one past life he was a brainwashed crusader, a master Muslim killer. In another life he was a warrior of Genghis Khan's army, hacking into everybody with his grand sword until he was hacked himself. I asked him: "Wasn't there a good atmosphere with your fellow soldiers?" "No", he said: "Every man for himself." His only friend was his sword. I hope I did a good job deprogramming him.

Contrary to natives with Pluto in the tenth house natives with Pluto in the eleventh house hate to take part in committees. They feel uneasy at conventions. At work the board meetings with staff and personnel are considered a hell. And they have a lot of arguments for it: 'It is theater. It is all cooked up before. Why spend hours discussing how to spend one dime? A waste of time and money.' When you tell them such meetings are socially necessary to stay in tune with each other and to get to know each other better they just gaze wide-eyed. They can't understand that there would be anybody who enjoys those meetings. No wonder natives with Pluto in the eleventh house get in problems for this attitude. Even if they hide their disgust people feel it.

Another pain in the ass for natives with Pluto in the eleventh house is going to a course. They only join a study group when they have to. Suppose they like astrology and study it. They don't go to an astrology workshop. Not over their dead body. They work it out all alone.

A lot of natives with Pluto in the eleventh house work with groups. Often they become a teacher in elementary school or high school. They stand in front of the class. They don't join the class. They control class. They are not a child. They are the teacher. The teacher is the leader so the distance stays. In most cases they make excellent teachers. The children in class are always on their mind. They are committed to their pupils. If the children start to pester you, you suffer sleepless nights how to work it out. And you will. That is the power. Being a teacher is healing for their soul. They work out their karma not to be afraid facing a crowd (or mob). Children are not that dangerous. Adults are worse. Most teachers with Pluto in the eleventh house are popular. On the other hand, having meetings in the teacher's board room (an adult mob) is of less joy. There they feel the underdog and are afraid to show themselves. There is the real tension. If there are problems in school it is with your co-teachers and not with the children.

If they don't become a teacher they'll be a steward for a travel company, a guide in a museum or something like that, leading the public through the place. They'll do that job with all their heart. They fear to lose control so they do their utter best. Again they don't join the group. They guide the groups, one after the other. How lonely. It is a way to transform their karma to get rid of their fears. The public they guide want to party. They don't bite. What a relief.

Natives with Pluto in the eleventh house are politically aware but not always that keen. They follow politics and get shocked by all the scandals. They get real angry about it. They are very critical. They hate party discipline. Rarely they go in politics. If they do they'll meet a lot of confrontation. They want a free role. Mostly they don't join the political game but from the sideline they watch and spit. They don't talk much about politics for fear their feelings rise up too high. Talking about politics they try to come up with an original opinion but somehow lose the main line. Reinventing politics is a hard thing to do. They have a burning protest in their heart but they hide it. Once in a while they show their indignation to an individual but they make sure it does not become public. Cynical they get in touch with politics through their job. For example: when you are a teacher you have got to be in line with the state educational program. I did some sessions with a teacher who got involved in grand trials with those 'educational programs'. She was the head teacher of the main school for uneducable children (fourteen year old scum walking around with stilettos). She had her own vision of helping those traumatized kids different from the one of the state department. She won all her lawsuits but was the big loser at the end. The educational community had put her on the black list. In a past life she committed suicide as a sixteen year old girl because they had laid out the rope for her and there was nowhere to go to. In this life she had a way out. She got a job as a politician and traveled throughout the country contacting all kinds of organizations. When she was home her husband was wailing that she was never home. She replied: "I am not your therapist. I am your wife!"

A lot of natives with Pluto in the eleventh house get in problems with society and its institutions. They don't seek it but it happens. An indignation strikes them and they have to fight for their rights. The defense escalates. It becomes a fight of David against Goliath, a fight against the hundred-headed dragon, a fight of Don Quichotte against the windmills of the institutions. Alone against the ultimate mafia: politics. It is all karma. Sometimes the indignation is so big they can't join society anymore. They simply can't bring it up anymore. They are not revolutionary. They have got the triple H status: Horrified, hopeless and helpless. They feel like outcasts, they act like outcasts and they get in problems like outcasts. Problems with the insurance companies, with the bankers, with the tax authorities and with all the regulations in general. When you explain to them that they should play the game better, they get furious.

During cracking Pluto in the eleventh house you are challenged to choose where you belong to. It is a solemn choice. For this organization and its people I stand for. You get in touch with an organization (a school, a charity fund, a hospital or whatever as long as it has a philosophy or ideology) and you decide to work for them. You decide: I am here to stay. Besides those people are real nice too. Cracking Pluto in the eleventh house means you plead loyalty to ...... deep out of your heart. Once you've done that you go for it and become a leading factor. That is the power of Pluto. Not as a leader but you carry the load.

If you have always worked for an organization whose rules you objected to or at least had some disagreement with, it will show. Suddenly all eyes are pointed at you and you have to speak out. There is an argument about what to do and they won't accept you standing on the sideline anymore. Or they wonder why you are absent so often from their meetings. Don't you like us? In most cases transiting Pluto runs through the second house which is a challenge for you to stand for your own values. Who are you working for? Are your set of values the same as mine. You have to speak out. Do I love you, my people, or not. If you don't you can pack your bags. What to do? What to say? It is like dying. If you are able to clear out the misunderstandings a new reality (transformation) begins and you will be a leader. If not, you don't like 'them' and you have to go, to create a new reality with another circle of people.

Cracking Pluto in the eleventh house means you find a circle of people you feel connected to. You join them on what they think and do and what they are living for. No division in public and private life. You give yourself with all your heart and energy. It will be seen and highly appreciated. When the power of Pluto in the eleventh house breaks through you actively join the group activities as a stimulator and generator. You are not a powerless subject. You are not the leader. You join in as equal. When you throw yourself in, you'll find out you will be supported. The proof comes when a conflict arises. All your pals stand by and support you. They won't let you down. Once you have gotten that security you have cracked Pluto in the eleventh house. Your friends are giving you energy instead of the other way around. Even if you have to be corrected yourself they don't let you down but correct you.

After cracking Pluto you know you are not alone. This bond could be of any sort. It could be professional. It could be non-commercial for a general goal. It could be a bond with your neighbors: fine people with a good heart for the community too. Or you join an astrology group organizing all kinds of lectures, conferences and newsletters to keep the group together. Or you join a group promoting medical herbs. Or you find your group in the sports center of your children. Or an environmental group. Whatever as long as it has a (political) goal too, a goal to share. For someone with Pluto in the eleventh house politics is always part of life. Don't deny it and don't overestimate it.

A silly (for outsiders) example of how to crack Pluto in the eleventh house: A man, happily married, ran a small grocery store in a giant shopping center selling delicatessens. "Good business but he could not hire in personnel because you know how expensive that is," as he always stated. (not of the writer: he is fooling himself. He has a Pluto in the eleventh house suspicion of personnel.) His shop, beautifully dressed up as a market stall, was always a full house. He was racing and running to serve his clients in time, but in vain. Weighing and packing all those delicatessens takes time. The waiting queue never stopped. He thought: 'They must hate me making them wait that long.' When he heard them sighing he thought it was out of irritation and he thought he would be lynched. At the age of cracking Pluto he started to mention it. 'Don't kill me. I am doing the best I can,' he shouted out. The all laughed. Finally his customers noticed it was not a joke. He meant it. They all explained they loved him. They were not angry with him. Visiting the shopping center they always stop by his shop. Not only for his products but also because they liked him so much. He was a nice man. First he did not believe it. A hundred thousand times they explained this to him. At the hundred thousand and first time he finally believed it. He was healed by his customers. A few years later he became the spokesman of the shopkeepers association. He always had the habit of visiting his colleagues after work to talk about the everyday problems in that shopping center. They all knew him very well (thanks to his Pluto in the eleventh house habit to have connections with all groups) and were glad to have him in the association. So that is how this man found peace of mind and solved his karmic problems with society, friends and loyalty. Not by a radical change but by change of attitude.

Mostly transiting Pluto stands in the second house during cracking Pluto. It means the transformation will be on the plane of your inner values in relation to work and money. Who are you working for? What kind of organization you work for? If you work for people you don't like or for an organization with a doubtful reputation the irritation will finally win over the money you make. At the end you stand for your social values and you change your job or even your profession and you meet new people you get along with better. In the beginning it is hard to give up your old securities and to start from zero but in the end it is the door to heaven.

Pluto in the twelfth house

Natives with Pluto in the twelfth house have a drive to be social and make the world a paradise and a fear to do so. The drive is a matter–of–course. The fear stems from over-sensitivity. A fear to be taken over by the situation feeling small, like a dwarf. Not all people are that good. They feel sorry for the awkward state of humanity. They have a double hearted relationship with the cosmic Providence. Knowing the cosmic laws is 'too big to handle', they feel victimized. Deep in their heart they protest against their lot. God is to blame. He created this world.

Natives with Pluto in the twelfth house have a fear of starting a relationship. Once they have gotten one they are afraid to be left alone. A fear of commitment and a separation anxiety. They are extremely sensitive. They feel their partner in all their nerves, they unify with their aura and become the other. They give their aura to the other. It feels like losing your soul. That is scary so you hold back. When you feel it happening you push your partner away to get yourself back again. Relating with someone with Pluto in the twelfth house often becomes an attracting and repulsing game. On and off …. On and off. Once you have got someone it becomes too much and you pull back. When a native with Pluto in the twelfth house gives himself to another it is forever. It is like a total surrender. Once that bond is made and the other person leaves you it is extremely painful. You gave your aura away and now he is gone with it. You can't forget him/her. It is like he/she is still with you although he is gone. You thought it was forever. That hurts. It is like dying.

Some natives with Pluto in the twelfth house decide not to relate at all. Why should you go through all the pain? Why should you connect yourself with someone when you know in advance it is temporary? That only hurts. And you don't want that. Natives with Pluto in the twelfth house feel an extreme sort of loneliness much worse than Saturn in the twelfth house.

This loneliness stems from past lives. In at least one past life you were torn loose from someone you loved dearly. You had a total togetherness and it was broken. Nobody wanted it but it happened. The pain was more than you could bear. In a past life your partner left you and you did not know why. He simply did not come back. For years you faithfully waited for him. At the end of your life you heard he lived in another country doing well in the Kings court. A special case was a woman that received the message of her partners death. Faithfully she believed she would meet him again in heaven. But it did not happen. He was not there. She expected him to be there and usually he should be there (that is the normal course) but he was not there. So she felt betrayed by Providence.

Feeling betrayed by Providence is another theme. A woman was a guiding angel before she incarnated. By Providence it was decided she should become human because so many people did not listen anymore to the angels. She should tell the people as their equal. But nobody listened to her and after a few lives in which she was brutally murdered she asked Providence to go back on their decision to change her into a human being. But no. This refusal was her reproach to God. I registered a past life of a man being a Buddhist monk. After a tough education he became a mendicant. Nobody listened to him. It was part of the culture to feed the monks . Nobody needed him. He felt betrayed by God making him a useless mendicant.

Natives with Pluto in the twelfth house feel lonely right from their birth like having lost something very beautiful. In their early years they always sense some queer or bad energies and they put up a wall against it. They expect to be born in a perfect world and find out it is not. The feeling of being left alone by everything and everybody sets in. Nobody knows. I registered the following in a re-birthing session: At the age of two the client suddenly got scared. She cried for her parents. Nobody showed up. She was completely alone and blamed her parents. The parents could not help it, not being there to help. You can't expect from a three year old toddler she will explain to you: "Mama, my basic problem is that I feel so lonely." Nobody notices because it is not talked about. It is hidden. There is no reason for it. Still there might be good reasons. Plutonic fears are felt and the abused can be merciless. For example with a violent father or a with a manipulative mother threatening she would leave when the child does not behave right. Basic thing is: a wall is constructed in the aura of the child as a protection against someone else's aura.

This wall becomes a problem in puberty when you fall in love with someone. The walls you constructed tumble down. That is scary. You give yourself to your lover unconditionally and then you find he takes over your aura. Your aura gets sucked away. You try to explain it but it is inexplicable. Having a lover means you have to withdraw regularly to recover, to regain yourself, to get back your own aura. You pull back to your own place and you don't want to see him for some days. The lover does not understand and insists on an explanation. You tell him: "Don't haunt me." Later you regret it. You constantly think about him because he is in your aura. You contact him again. Next you give away your aura again only to pull back again. The story repeats itself. This game might result in a sadomasochistic attracting and repulsing situation. Your love affair becomes a flashing light. On and off, on and off.

The relating and separation anxiety can manifest in several ways:

1) After a few tries you decide relating is too troublesome and you prefer to be single. You can't open up to the other out of self-protection. It is too big to handle. Often the first love is with someone who is troublesome (drug problems or mental problems) and needs help. (That is the beauty of Pluto in the twelfth house: it means a very social attitude …. too social to handle.) You tried but in vain and after this love you decide a relationship costs more than it is worth. No more relations.

2) You hang on to a fake relationship with someone you can't reach. You deliberately choose a love affair when you know in advance it will not work out. This person lives far away in another town or country and by misfortune it is impossible to meet each other. Or you love a crazy nut impossible to handle. Or someone who is lonely like yourself but rejects all contact. (again this social attitude.) Or you love someone who is married and of course that can't be. What a tragedy to have such a lot. 'It is like it is'. You really are the victim. But it is all fake. You create it yourself out of fear of commitment.

3) You have many short-lived relations. Like a tarantula you dive into a bed with someone and the next day you don't want to see him/her anymore. When you are too

long together you get musty. You feel drowned in the aura of the other and need to free yourself from it. First you tell him you want to be on your own and not be bothered. Next you tell him to bug off.

4) Your love life is a flashing light to the despair of your lover. You have a relationship. You don't want to live together. You see him only once in a while.

5) You have a lover although you can't tear down your walls. You get persuaded and stay with him and you suppress the feeling of losing yourself. Practically you live together but still you keep your own apartment. The relation is halfhearted. You keep in mind that it is always possible he will leave you and that is how you arrange your life. You have your own bank account, your own apartment, your own job, all set to go. If it gets to the point of breaking up you can leave him on your own terms. Even in your marriage certificate you brought in a clause to secure you in case he would leave you. That way it would not hurt that much.

6) You give yourself totally to your partner as an assurance he will not leave you. You feel so small you need someone else's aura and strength. Having a relation is a rescue for your loneliness. You feel a strong bond but also insecurity. You hand in your soul and become your partner. You hang on to your lover for dear life. You expect your love to be eternal by giving yourself totally. You want certainty he does not leave you. When you get signals he would be able to leave you get tensed up. Either you start to provoke arguments or you turn into an abject slave. As an abject slave you do everything to keep your lover in order to not be left alone. Without your partner you are nothing. You

hang on to him/her and humiliate yourself on the psychic, emotional and sexual level. You take on a masochistic attitude. You make yourself pitiful. You do the craziest things to make your partner happy. "Beat me, beat me, if that will make you happy." All this does nothing to earn your partner's respect. Things get worse and at the cracking of Pluto he does leave you despite (or because of) all your humiliations. And that is hard. That hurts. That is mean. It is unbearable. That is how cruel the cosmos is. It is hell. It is mourning. It is awful hard to pull yourself together. You can't forget how mean he/she was. Over and over again you explained to him how much you loved him and all his friends. Merciless he left you. Your separation anxiety became a self-fulfilling prophecy. At the end he did not deserve your love. The only way is to get yourself (your aura) back again and continue your life, realizing it is not the end of the world.

Some natives with Pluto in the twelfth house provoke their lover for as long as they can. First they say: "Go then, go then, if you are happier with someone else." At the end he goes and you can say: 'See. He left me. I always knew he would.' Or they are suspicious their lover is adulterous but he is not. Unconsciously they aim for a break up. In an untraceable tricky way it is always the partner who is to blame. Everybody will know what a bastard he is. He pushed you aside like a piece of dirt.

7) You give yourself totally to your partner as it should be. You hide your fears that he will leave you although it is giving you sleepless nights. By the time of cracking Pluto by some dramatic event you find out he has not left you and he never will. What a relief. Your karmic problem is solved.

Cracking Pluto in the twelfth house means you make a firm decision. Either you commit yourself or you don't commit at all without any middle way. If you don't and you've found out it is easier to find peace of mind when you are alone you stick to that. It means you commit yourself to the inexhaustible cosmic source of light and care. It is a cosmic consciousness. The light will guide you for the rest of your life. Some truly become deeply religious. They build an altar in their home in close contact with their guiding angel or they join a religious group. Others don't call it a religion. They simply get the experience that they feel better when they are alone. When they come home from work they don't want a wife or husband hanging around. That is how they feel good and that is what they choose for themselves. Something has changed inside and you can bear life alone. Moreover if you, after many years, meet by course of Providence someone you can start a lasting relationship with, your inner light stays as your guiding power. It means you don't get lost anymore in the aura of your partner. You have grown some backbone.

During cracking Pluto in the twelfth house you stand for the decision to commit yourself or not. Cracking Pluto in the twelfth house means to tear down your walls. It means you decide to stop this half-heartedness. It means you will be clear about your decision: IN or OUT. If you meet someone and choose to live together you faithfully and unconditionally give yourself to your partner. No more pulling the rope anymore. Once you've decided he is in, you stick to it. Once you've decided he is out, you stick to it. It is all about reliability.

When your love life is a flashing light or projected on an unreachable goal a climax will come when transiting Pluto squares your natal Pluto. When you waver too long your partner might say: "Now it is out for good. I won't let you push me away each time. I won't come back again." What you were so afraid of happened. Deep in your heart you know it was you who could not surrender. It's your own fault. But you play the victim in a masochistic fantasy. Cutting the emotional ties is extremely hard. He still has part of your aura and somehow you have got to get it back. The problem is: nobody ever learned how to do that.

One of the bad habits of natives with Pluto in the twelfth house is playing the victim. Playing the victim is complaining. By complaining about somebody you are discrediting them. This way you set people up against each other. That is not cosmic love.

When you live together while not being able to tear down your walls your partner will feel it. He feels lonely meeting your wall. You hide in an iron shell. You are out of reach. You expect him to be a perfect being all in tune with the cosmos but you notice he is not. By the high sensitivity of Pluto in the twelfth house it hurts you deep in your heart. You keep on nagging about what is wrong. Your partner should be like you want him as though he is your possession. You tie your partner down with an iron hook. For example you try to force your lover to make all kinds of promises. If he disappoints you, it comes in hard, and it is you who threatens to leave as a power game. I don't know about you if you are like that ..... Don't disappoint me again. Your partner does his best but cannot prevent disappointing you again. By the time of cracking Pluto either you free yourself from your shell or a divorce will follow. Finally your partner gives up and leaves. Next you play the victim that he has left you. Cracking Pluto is to understand how it happened.

Another thing some natives with Pluto in the twelfth house should learn is you can't possess somebody. You can share your life, melt into one another but you can't possess someone. The relation can turn into a sadomasochistic struggle to possess or to be possessed. It is loneliness that compels you to want to have somebody for reasons of security. Eventually this will not work out. So if you are left alone and you have to crack Pluto you have to realize this love will never return in the same way and with the same person. If you meet a new person it will be in a different way. Often in an unexpected way. If love shows up again you just say 'yes' to the situation and go with the flow as it comes, unconditionally. You throw all your fears and hesitations in the garbage and go for it. That's the way. Once I did a regression session with someone with Pluto in the twelfth house. She was left alone and treated as an abject slave. She was trapped in a barrel metaphorically speaking. During the session she realized she could not open up to her husband and for this reason he left her. She met her guiding angel, being a woman, giving her warmth and the opportunity to hand over her anger and sorrow. Her guiding angel emphasized she could not stay with her forever because she also had other people to care for. But if she is really in trouble she could call on this angel. In other words: he guiding angel is not her possession although she is hers.

Another rather harmless phenomena of Pluto in the twelfth house is not being able to say goodbye in a proper way. The moment you say goodbye you unconsciously think it is forever. You hold in or exaggerate. Or you choke and freeze completely or you start a set of complicated rituals. At the last moment you realize there are so many things you forgot to say. When the train leaves the station ….. you collapse. Even if you know for sure there will be a next meeting it still feels like it is forever.

A lot of parents with Pluto in the twelfth house get tensed up when their children leave home. They realize their child has grown up and has to go for himself. They don't wait until the kid discovers for himself that he wants to leave to make his own living. They plan it in advance. Years before they prepare the child that he will leave their parental home. "Mama can't care for you forever. It is like it is." But for the child it is premature. The child feels dismissed or even kicked out. Suppose your child is in the senior class and plans to go to college in another town. A Pluto in the twelfth house reaction is to arrange everything for your child in advance. Where he is going to live, with whom he is going to be ..... to protect their child from the uncertain ways of Providence. And you want him to come home so badly. When he comes home you are always discussing his way of living. As a result your child is reluctant to visit you. He doesn't visit you anymore. Maybe once a year at Christmas time. Sometimes cracking Pluto in the twelfth house means your child indeed winds up in the gutter having alcohol and drug problems and there is nothing you can do .... but to accept it and be there when needed. The thing is: natives with Pluto in the twelfth house are super caring and social but sometimes it is overdone.

Some natives with Pluto in the twelfth house are mad at God. It starts when they get their first grim experiences. They don't trust the world anymore. A silly game of attracting and repulsing sets in. This happens in your relationships, at your job, in courses and to everyone you give your trust to. The world is a bad place and people are crazy. It is as it is. Just look around. They protest the plan of creation. They long for paradise and a perfect world but by God's Providence it is not. It is all about good and bad. In fact they pretend to know better than God. What sometimes happens is: they choose for the bad side. If you cannot beat them join them. They hang out with criminals, getting a piece of their cake and they pretend to be criminal themselves. It is all fake. They don't dare. They pretend to be bad. They cooperate with bad people as a lifestyle. Once I had a reading with someone with Pluto in the twelfth house who worked in a SM nightclub. She read my Moon node book and started a discussion. "Sebastian, you claim in your books the good ones finally will win in the end." I grumbled: "It is all about how you define good and bad." She continued: "I don't believe that. If you are mean enough you'll get everything you want. If you are a goody-goody you get nothing." "Yes," I replied, "winner takes it all. How many bodyguards do you need?" She continued: "You write in your book that if you are mean and cruel and you take joy in repressing, exploiting and power abuse you will pay the bill in a next life." I was trembling by her fierceness but stayed cool: "I didn't write that literally but you might conclude that." "Well", she said, "I don't believe that and it is not according to my observations." End of the discussion. Still she did a regression session with me and occasionally she wiped a tear away repeating with a low voice, "it is like it is", not being able to explain what 'it is'.

The basic problem of Pluto in the twelfth house is loneliness. With great comic insight you see the rain of tears, the unhappiness all around. There is no language for it. There is a drive to help and care. Before cracking Pluto you don't know how. Feeling like a dwarf you look up to the big world. Your sensitivity makes you afraid and powerless. You look for a giant for help. He has to reaffirm this insight. You are testing out, manipulating and negotiating to hear what you want to hear. And if not, you fall back into loneliness. During cracking Pluto this will alter. You find the words yourself (transiting Pluto in the third house). The feeling of being small will be transformed into giving power and love from inner wisdom.

Cracking Pluto in the twelfth house is all about realizing your own world of illusion. Your illusions are like a straitjacket. The straitjacket of the thought that 'it is like it is' and you can't do anything. The straitjacket of your expectations, your own will and what you want to have so badly. The illusion of your own plan of life not matching Providence. The illusion to control everything in your life, your partner to begin with. Cracking Pluto in the twelfth house is breaking up with those illusions by talking. Talking (transiting Pluto in the third house) is the way. Instead of hiding in lonely fatalism you should say yes to the things you meet on your path. It begins with talking. You open up to Providence and let happen what has got to happen. You start to take life as it comes. So if you live in miserable conditions don't blame others anymore and do something about it.

In the end a native with Pluto in the twelfth house can get hard times when all your acquaintances are old and one after the other fades out and passes on. Although you know everybody will die eventually (in fact it is the only real certainty you have), it is still hard. After they've died you miss them. Don't feel sorry for yourself or the surviving relatives. The deceased is back home. In this time it is urgent to pick up your cosmic knowledge and crack Pluto again. With this knowledge you can do a good job in death coaching. A lot of people are afraid to die. Dying is no fun. Be there and help them with passing over. That's very important. Being there without sobbing is enough.

With the strength of Pluto you'll be of great help for everybody before, during and after the funeral for the dying and the living and the cosmos in general.